D1460518

Dear Christophe,

Happy 24th Belated Birthday!

You are THE only Connoisseur of fine cigars that I know. I hope this book will only heighten & develop your profound knowlege on THE subject. I know what you're like with Rubik's Cubes & such so this does not mean memorising each page inside out. Haha. To borrow from THE Pink Floyd song, "Have a Cigar"

"You're Gonna Go Far,
    You're Gonna Fly High"

Tradition » Passion » Perfection

Colin Ganley is co-chief editor of the *European Cigar Journal*, the largest cigar magazine in Europe. Born in Minnesota, Colin is now a researcher at Saint Antony's College, Oxford University. Alongside his regular column, 'Collector's Corner', about vintage and collectible cigars, he writes for cigar publications, including *Cigar Snob* magazine, and runs the website www.cigarresearch.com.

FROM NEIL, YOUR DEAREST FRIEND

& COTTON EMPEROR

Conceived and produced by
Elwin Street Productions
144 Liverpool Road
London N1 1LA
www.elwinstreet.com

Hardie Grant Books (Australia)
658 Church St
Richmond
Victoria 3121
www.hardiegrant.com.au

Hardie Grant Books (UK)
34–35 Southhampton Street
London WC2E 7HF
www.hardiegrant.co.uk

ISBN: 978-174270171-4

Illustrations: Tonwen Jones

Picture credits:
Alamy: p. 17, 79, 101; Corbis: p. 45, 63

Printed in China

CIGARS

Colin Ganley

hardie grant books
MELBOURNE · LONDON

Contents

Why be a snob about cigars?

A cigar can be easily ruined by careless hands; the home humidor can become a coffin for premium cigars; and even if you avoid the common pitfalls, as prices rise, it is the knowledgeable connoisseur who is rewarded for his shrewd selection of the best hand-crafted beauties.

These days it seems that everyone is developing expertise in one of their passions. Whether we focus on our clothing, food, drink or smoke, information abounds. All of these products have become highly specialised, and our daily sources of enjoyment can be heightened by gaining a deeper knowledge of these products. Industry leaders have written volumes of literature to explain the intricacies of producing and customising our daily consumables, and cigars are no different.

When it comes to cigars, understanding the difference between regions and brands, and being able to recognise true quality, can increase your appreciation of the experience. At all prices, cigars that shine brilliantly can be found. The most refined cigars, and cigars with invaluable pedigree can be found at auction or on the top shelves at cigar lounges and premium tobacconists. New cigar makers breaking in to the market offer lower-priced gems that are undervalued due to anonymity.

The world of cigars has grown since the early 1990s. Top-quality cigars are being produced by scores of makers. Some are in the Caribbean heart of production while others are further afield. But with thousands of cigars on the market, most normal people, even those with a real passion for fine cigars, will not be able to sample all of them. A sharp review of available cigars reveals that not all cigars on offer are worth an enthusiast's time. But with these thousands of options, how is one to sort the sugar from the stones?

Even the enthusiast who has time to smoke such variety has little energy left over to dive deeply into the peculiarities of each country and maker. And anyone with a genuine interest in cigars will know that the sampling of a cigar is not just in the smoking; the story behind it can be as intriguing as its taste and aroma.

This guide seeks to assist you in your pursuit of such knowledge. The world's best cigar makers create diamonds. Some are dull while others are brilliant. Throughout this guide, the uniqueness of each maker and country are brought to the fore, highlighting and recommending their finest products. All of the cigars included in this book have been carefully selected as the finest products available to help you in your passion.

However, a few are of particular note, and have been highlighted as a Le Snob Essential – this is the shining example of that particular maker's creations. It is recommended for superior taste and aroma, as well as trustworthy and consistent craftsmanship, and will reveal the maker's best work. Peppered throughout the book, they are the ones most highly recommended to include in your collection. Each is rolled by masters of the *chaveta*. The blends smoke coolly, with balanced flavours and unique contributions to the lexicon of tobacco tastes.

In short, this is a guide for the experienced cigar enthusiast. For one who enjoys premium cigars and is thirsty for knowledge. It reaches across the Caribbean from the powerful tobaccos of Central America, through Cuba's rich aromas, to the Dominican Republic's finesse to show you the finest cigars available today, and why it is worth being a snob about the cigars you choose to smoke.

In this book, cigars have been grouped into categories based upon the country of origin. The manufacturers and brands are not always based in that country, often the headquarters are elsewhere, but the tobacco itself is produced in that country.

In the case of Cuba, the uniqueness of these cigars is self-explanatory. Cuban cigars are all made according to traditional methods and of exclusively Cuban tobacco. While cigars from other countries are often made of tobaccos from many origins, each country has its unique practices, makers and tobaccos. These differences provide you with a starting point for understanding the unique identities of each of these country designations.

» Fundamentals

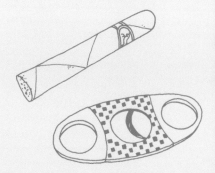

Appreciating fine cigars

Cigar enjoyment takes more into consideration than simply the beauty of the box. As with products such as wine or whisky, enjoyment is based not simply upon the quality of raw materials – the construction is vital, knowing whether a cigar was produced by a machine or hand made by highly trained artisans. The finest cigars are handmade, long filler cigars, blended by experts with high-quality premium tobacco. It is only cigars of this type that will be profiled in this volume.

Cigar wrappers

Cigars today speak from their wrappers. The outermost leaf often reveals the philosophy of the creator. In the classic style, many premium cigars wear flawless, smooth and uniformly coloured wrappers. These expensive leaves impart flavour but also set the expectations of the smoker. A Davidoff cigar is always cloaked in gorgeous rich attire. An expectation of refinement is warranted when looking at these and similar cigars.

Dark, textured, oily and rough wrappers can now be found on such illustrious cigars as the Tatuaje Black Label. These leaves would previously not have been considered to be of wrapper quality. But they speak of the maker's preference for bold taste and have a beauty that is not traditional.

Despite this variety of wrapper appearance, quality can still be ascertained by looking at and touching premium cigars. No matter the wrapper appearance, a cigar should be evenly filled. This can be felt when a cigar is squeezed between the fingers from foot to head. Hard spots and soft spots point to shoddy workmanship and suggest poor smoking performance.

Taste and aroma

The ultimate test of a cigar is its taste and aroma. No matter who makes a cigar, they aim to provide supreme qualities in the mouth and nose. Rich and chocolaty or mild and spicy, cigars are designed to deliver a pleasing taste.

A cigar's taste may be more suited to the evening hours and a distilled companion. Some cigars are nutty and pair well with coffee. Its taste profile does not determine its quality but rather its identity. Quality is determined by the palatability of the taste and the fermentation of the tobacco.

Know the history

In the pattern of all connoisseur products, the story of your cigar is of some value. Cigars, because of where they are produced, have some of the most romantic stories of all consumables. Revolutions, hurricanes and business intrigues provide a rich background to every smoke, and can heighten your appreciation.

It is possible to smoke cigars from before and after the revolutions in Cuba and Nicaragua. Generations of cigar makers have passed the torch in the Dominican Republic and Honduras. These events often have quite an effect on the production and taste of the cigars, so it is worth knowing a little about these factors as each reveals more about the identity of the cigar in your hand.

Types of cigars

Cigars are categorised in many different ways. The increasing variety of cigar shapes, tobaccos used, prices and recommendations allows you to think of your cigars in dozens of ways. For example, strong, medium or light cigars refers to the amount of nicotine and thus aggressiveness in a cigar.

A cigar enthusiast, however, is probably more interested in the flavours, duration of smoke and complexity than he is in the 'strength' of a cigar. Does the cigar have flourishes like a tapered end, a shaggy foot or a pigtail head? What cigar will complement my peaty single malt Scotch? These are among the questions you are more likely to ask.

Shape and size

In Cuba, the different cigar sizes are called *vitolas*. Each *vitola* has specific dimensions. These fall into the categories of slim, hearty and robust. Since cigars have been produced outside of Cuba, producers have invented new *vitolas* and even renamed classic ones.

Most cigars produced today are categorised as a *parejo*, which means that the cigar has straight sides and a rounded head. The Panatela, Lancero, Reyes, Petit Corona, Corona, Corona Gorda, Churchill, Robusto and Double Corona all fall in that category.

Some special cigars, rolled by the best rollers, are made with tapered heads and feet or with bulged middles. These are called *figurados*. The most common of these is called the Torpedo. It has straight sides but it tapers to a point at the head, like a military torpedo. Salomon cigars represent one of the most curvaceous shapes. It tapers to a point at the head but near the foot it bulges before it nearly closes at the foot in the shape of a nipple.

Smoking time

An important consideration in cigar length is how long it will take to smoke:

7" or more After dinner, if you have the time, preferences often shift to long cigars. The Churchill, Double Corona and Lancero are rewards for a successfully completed day.

Churchill

Corona Gorda

Corona

Double Corona

Lancero

Robusto

Canonazo

Salomon

Torpedo

Standard 5–6" and 50 ring gauge Today's enthusiast more often gravitates to the Robusto, and its brethren, for a break of about an hour. For some reason, wide cigars of five to six inches are now the most popular. **Under 5" and 48 ring gauge** Also gaining popularity is a classic size, the Petit Corona, or Perla, or other short and slender smokes. These cigars are finding their places in the busy lives of today's connoisseur.

Popular *vitolas*

Below are some of the most popular *vitolas*, with their lengths and their ring gauge (a measurement of its diameter expressed in 64ths of an inch).

Slim *vitolas*

Panatela	4⅝" x 34
Laguito #1 (Lancero)	7¼" x 38
Reyes	4⅜" x 40
Petit Corona (Mareva)	5⅛" x 42

Hearty *vitolas*

Corona	5⅝" x 42
Corona Gorda	5⅝" x 46
Torpedo	6⅛" x 52 (smaller at head)

Robust *vitolas*

Robusto (Rothschild)	4⅞" x 50
Double Corona	7⅝" x 49
Salomon	7" x 57 (tapered at both ends)

How to smoke a cigar

Knowing how to cut and light cigars is part of the essential prerequisite knowledge for smoking a cigar, as is inhaling and ashing.

Cutting a cigar

To ensure that a cigar does not unravel in your mouth, it is essential to cut it cleanly and not too aggressively. The most common reason for a cigar coming undone is too deep a cut. Since cigars are held together at the head by tobacco extending just a fraction of an inch down the body of the cigar, it is essential to not remove too much of the head.

A standard and optimal cut is done by one or two blades which remove the cap. Ideally, a cigar's head is only slightly trimmed. The end of the cigar, once cut, should reveal a flat surface of freshly cut leaves and none of the cap should remain. Any portion of the cap remaining on the head of the cigar will collect smoke and saliva and most often will create a bitter liquid reservoir. It is telling that fancy cutters such as V-cut, fish-eye and others are not used by cigar makers. The only exception is the punch cutter, which is best used when the opening it reveals is slightly smaller than the diameter of the cigar.

Lighting a cigar

Lighting is supremely important in the early taste of the cigar. Damage done at lighting can be rectified by touch-ups and metered puffing, but it is best to avoid such problems in the first instance. Either

» Gathering leaves

Creating a highly complex premium cigar requires
leaf from many farms in many parts of the tobacco-
cultivating world. In order to acquire leaf from far
afield, cigar makers can either leave their factories
and travel extensively, or rely on others to bring the
leaf to them.

A century ago, brokers would buy tobacco from
farms around the island of Cuba and bring it to
Havana to sell to the factories. Today, brokers buy
tobacco from Africa, Asia, South America, North
America and all around the Caribbean. They bring
the tobacco to warehouses near factories in Santiago,
Esteli and Danli. Cigar makers then visit the brokers
and purchase the unfinished tobacco and have it
sent to their factories for final fermentation and
ultimately rolling.

butane lighters or wooden matches are recommended to light a cigar.

Some of the worst offenders are those who light cigars for us. When they light your cigar, watch them to ensure that they practise the same care you would. No matter what sort of fuel they use, the visible portion of the flame should not touch the tobacco. The best heat and least amount of gas exists at the tip of the flame, where it becomes invisible to the human eye. The two chief problems of lighting, charring and overheating, can both be prevented by using small flames and not allowing the visible flame to touch the tobacco.

Smoking a cigar

You should smoke slowly, not drawing too frequently, and don't inhale the cigar smoke – you can enjoy a cigar's flavour and body without inhaling. To increase the breadth of flavours you experience, try the retrohaling technique (see page 67).

Ashing a cigar

Cigars do not need to be repeatedly tapped for ash as you would with a cigarette, and doing so may knock out the cherry. A quality, well-rolled cigar should be able to sustain an ash 2 or 3 inches long. Generally you should ash it when the ash is about an inch long. Gently press the end of the cigar into the bottom of an ashtray, and rotate the cigar to ensure it breaks off evenly.

The creation of a cigar

Tobacco, especially that used for cigars, tends to be grown in tropical regions. Once the leaves have been harvested, they are then left to be dried in 'tobacco barns', for approximately two months before going through the fermentation stage. It is during this process that the flavour and aroma of a leaf start to emerge, and levels of ammonia, resin and nicotine and other unwanted substances, are reduced. The fermented tobacco is then stored for maturation, which can take months or years depending on the quality required. The aged leaves are sent on to the factories where they are graded for quality, size and colour, and are then ready for selection and to be handrolled into premium cigars.

Role of the master blender

Conducting the orchestra of cigar making are the blenders, often called the Master Blenders, usually a team of the most highly skilled *tabaqueros* in a factory. It often includes the owner, the head of production and the most respected tasters in the rolling gallery. The Master Blenders keep a cigar company in business. They are responsible for ensuring that your favourite cigar tastes the same from year to year and box to box. They maintain consistency and create blends for new cigars. These are the people creating and tasting the enigmatic white-banded cigars (see page 20).

The blenders stand at the gateway between the tobacco and the connoisseur. Their skill is in artfully selecting leaves from different varieties, countries, regions, farms and primings to creat new blends and flavours. They are the chef in a factory, determining the recipe, and so the taste and appearance of the cigars. Every tobacco that arrives at the factory is tasted several times. Once it is deemed suitable for rolling, it may be selected by the blenders to create a certain taste profile.

While these experts are seldom recognised, they are among the most skilled and essential workers in the cigar-making process. The consistency of a brand and the quality of a taste should be, in large part, credited to a factory's blenders.

Blender's art

In any innovative cigar factory, scores of plain white-banded cigars can be found. The future of the company may be determined by these unassuming sticks: they are the sample blends created by the factory's blenders.

The white-banded cigar is one of very few cigars made with a test blend. The cigars are evaluated by a factory's decision makers. If the blend is good enough, it might earn a brand name.

Balance, complexity, taste, aroma, burn and appearance must all be monitored in the blends by the Master Blender. Only when the balance is correct, do the white bands have a chance of becoming glossy bands.

Develop your own taste

Everyone knows that a savoury steak au poivre tastes different from a sweet crème brûlée. But can cigars taste so different? Cigars' similar appearances fool amateurs, but the expert taster knows that different coronas can taste as different as lemonade and chocolate pudding.

There is a wide variety of flavours across the many different available brands and products. The flavour comes from both the wrapper and the filler tobacco that has been used. Generally, it is down to individual taste and choice, but the range of options can be daunting.

Developing the skill of cigar tasting requires a bit more effort than simply smoking boxes of cigars. Anyone can determine whether they like a cigar or not. All that judgement requires is comparison of flavours against what is liked and what is not. To compare cigars smoked at different times is a somewhat more difficult endeavour. Even more challenging is to compare hundreds of cigars, produced years apart and smoked at different times, under different circumstances. Nonetheless, this ability is highly valuable and worth striving to achieve.

Quality over branding

To know what cigar is most enjoyable, is to be able to look beyond product marketing and price, to appreciate the product for its quality alone. Anyone who has mastered tasting knows what will be enjoyed and what provides the best value. In order to master this skill, there are a few tricks of the trade that are used by blenders in training, magazine cigar reviewers and other professionals in the business and hobby.

Two at a time

One of the most revealing exercises for cigar novices is a strange-looking practice, tasting two cigars at once. Rarely will an enthusiast do this in a trendy cigar divan – it looks indulgent and out of place. However, it is a useful practice when identifying the different flavours in the cigars, and the direct comparison of tastes shows the smoker the vast range of flavours which can be extracted from the noble tobacco leaf.

Factory visits

Another way to improve your tasting abilities is to go to the source. Because wine and spirits are created in large containers, the taste is uniform from bottle to bottle. Tobacco leaves, being solid, are much harder to blend. Leaves can vary from one to the other and so does the taste.

There is no better way to grasp the difficulty of the task and to appreciate the variety of tastes than to experience production. Taste a strong leaf from Esteli, a spicy leaf from the Dominican Republic; a savoury leaf from Vinales (Cuba); and a sweet leaf from Brazil. Then combine them. Do you like the blend? Now tweak the blend until you have found the perfect combination of flavours. This exercise is not only a lesson in the difficulty of cigar blending, it also reveals the variety of tastes available in premium

Words from the wise

Reinhold C. Widmayer Editor,
European Cigar Cult Journal

» Tasting kits and practice

Critically tasting cigars is hard and highly skilled work. Everyone tastes, but very few people can taste at the level of an expert cigar taster, or food or drink taster for that matter.

Tasting cigars is a skill that you can develop, however. On the market you can find aroma kits that have tens of unique-smelling oils and other substances. With regular practice you can go through all of these and train your nose, by smelling the different aromas, to identify what it is sensing, so that you can recognise them when smoking a cigar.

Of course you don't have to buy a kit for the purpose – you can just gather spices, fruits, woods and other familiar and common aromas associated with cigars.

It takes a lot of work to become very good at describing cigar tastes and aromas. But it can be done with regular practice.

tobacco and how those tastes change when paired with tobaccos of other origins.

Understanding the blend

Why is it useful to know about tobacco blending when tasting? For the same reason it can be useful to know things like how cakes are baked when eating one. To know that tobaccos are not thoroughly fermented is akin to knowing that a cake is undercooked. Manufacturers have different styles. Some prefer to leave tobaccos less fermented. Some prefer to make cigars which are sweet and simple. This understanding of style allows the taster to pinpoint the reason that a cigar tastes a certain way, whether desired or not.

Organised tasting

More and more cigar events are being organised by cigar manufacturers, retailers and other professionals. While most events are organised to sell cigars, they can also be a useful way to gain insight into the way professionals taste cigars. The professionals who lead the tastings will usually reveal all of their techniques at these events, so you can check out things such as whether they smell the tobacco before lighting the stick, how quickly they smoke and how they describe the different tastes.

Tasting terminology

When tasting cigars, we often rely upon familiar descriptions of taste and aroma. At cigar tasting events, people with different backgrounds describe flavours in the ways that are most comfortable for them. What one person describes as vegetal, another person may call acidic. By listening to different perspectives, one cannot help but enhance their knowledge of how tastes are recognised. Some of the terms you may come across in the description of cigar flavours include spicy, peppery, sweet, harsh, burnt, earthy, cocoa, roasted, aged, nutty, creamy, cedar, oak, chewy and fruity.

Critical smoking

The key to improving your cigar-tasting ability is to simply be critical, focusing on the taste and aroma. The above techniques are all excellent ways to focus your attention.

Critical tasting opens many doors in the cigar hobby. It allows you to select cigars that deliver the most value, regardless of price and provenance. Not only this, but cigars are often consumed with liquid friends. Best pairings can only really be determined when a person thoroughly understands the taste of their cigars. For more information on pairing drinks with cigars see page 125.

Cigar etiquette

Cigar culture has changed. In the past, it seemed that cigars could only be enjoyed at the proper place and time. No longer. Today's cigar lovers are unabashedly puffing their treasured sticks in plain sight both day and night. Something has dramatically changed.

UNIQUE » RARE » LITTLE-KNOWN » ULTIMATE **Snob**

Make your own blend Growing tobacco is much more difficult than growing something like a tomato. Since it takes many years and scores of people to make a commercial cigar, it is almost impossible to create your own cigar from scratch.

But with the right connections or a strong desire, you can, to a degree, create a customised cigar by skipping the tobacco growing; just blend and roll. Blending tobaccos to create a unique-tasting cigar is complicated but some manufacturers will allow you to try your hand at it.

The experience is intoxicating and overwhelming. Matching tobaccos, the sweet with the spicy, the rough filler and smooth wrapper, is harder than it looks. But at the end, the product you have created can be compared with the work of the masters.

Smoking rooms

Just a decade ago, following a sumptuous dinner, your host would bring out a selection of premium cigars, golden accoutrements and vintage port. You would savour the exclusive bonding experience as much as the cigar. Smoking a premium cigar in your car or at a casual restaurant seemed uncouth.

Today, cigar passionados are rarely able to smoke in fine restaurants. Bans are pervasive. Whether at home or when travelling, you have probably encountered restrictive smoking bans.

While the disappearance of smoking rooms in restaurants and clubs is a cultural loss, the culture of cigar enjoyment has not disappeared. It is now just a little more public.

Those who continue to indulge in these handcrafted masterpieces seem to have adopted a new attitude towards cigars. No longer does a cigar represent the embarrassment of riches. Much like wine, cigars are publicly appreciated for their craftsmanship, history and ability to deliver pleasure in a small package.

Bands and labels

For decades it has been honorable to remove the band, or label, from your cigar when smoking. 'I don't want to be ostentatious' a cigar smoker might say. The usual reason for removal was to hide the marking of the cigar's proud pedigree. A social cigar smoker might argue that there is no reason to have hierarchy during the bonding exercise of cigar smoking.

Concerns about these displays of gilded cigar bands slid to the back burner as more cigar makers have established themselves as true artists in the craft of cigar making. Different cigar brands no longer sit on a well-defined ladder of quality. Instead, each brand has a story to tell. Some speak of a century of tradition while others represent the emigrant's pursuit of passion after leaving his native land.

Rather than being a symbol of superiority, the cigar bands now present an opportunity for cigar enthusiasts to engage one another on the topic of 'that cigar'.

Common appreciation

Strangers, who would never have met in a private smoking room, now have regular meetings in cigar stores, lounges and clubs around the world. We are now all members of an inclusive club. The only price of membership is that which you pay for a hand-rolled cigar.

It is with a certain degree of sadness that we say goodbye to well-used smoking rooms and the gentlemanly tradition of brand modesty. But we have replaced these traditions with a much richer dialogue. Relieved of our propriety, we may now discuss those embossed and painted bands, the artists who nurtured the leaves and the sublime pleasure we derive from our well-cared-for treasures.

» Cuba

Cigars and Cuban identity

Just saying the words, Havana Cuba, accelerates the heart. It conjures images of 1950s Cadillacs, Spanish colonial architecture, rhythmic nightlife, rum and jazz. Whether it is revolutionaries, mafiosos, cabarets or swaying green fields of tobacco that come to mind, the thought of Cuba is evocative.

In any imagined Cuban scene, cigars are present. Beaches, nightclubs, farms and factories on the island all contain a contented Cuban, smoking a cigar. The image of the cigar is so tied to the country's identity that it proliferates the country's art, theatre and even politics. Cigars are even given as diplomatic gifts by the Cuban state.

Cigar factories

During the late 19th and early 20th centuries, cigar factories popped up across Havana, Cuba's capital city. At its peak there were over one hundred. As the twentieth century advanced, companies were purchased and merged until the majority of popular cigar brands were owned by just a few companies.

After the Cuban Revolution, led by Fidel Castro, many small manufacturers decided to close shop and either change occupation or leave the country. The largest factories came under the management of the new government and the brands continued to be produced. The brands we see today, such as Partagas and Montecristo, among others, went through this transition. Many of the manufacturers that did emigrate re-established their brands elsewhere, the result being that occasionally the same brand name is used by two independent companies, such as Partagas cigars, one of which is Cuban, while the other is based in the Dominican Republic.

Habanos

Consolidation continued after the Revolution as the state brought all production under one corporate manager called TabaCuba. TabaCuba now manufactures all hand-rolled cigars in Cuba and an assortment of factories around the country, most near Havana. Scattered export and distribution channels were also consolidated and are handled by a company known today as Habanos S.A.

The mystique of the Cuban cigar

The Cuban cigar owns the title of the world's first premium cigar. Tobacco was grown and smoked in Cuba even when Christopher Columbus first arrived. Although Cuba was not the only place where tobacco was grown, what happened in Cuba, and with Cuban tobacco, created the modern cigar industry.

From the spread of the European trading companies, such as the East India Company, tobacco was planted from the Caribbean to Japan. It was a global crop by the end of the seventeenth century. While sailors and city folk puffed cigars of various origins, it was Havana cigars that were most desired from the earliest days.

Charles Graves, in his 1930 book *Cigars and The Man* described seven categories of cigar, based upon occasion. Less interesting or cheap cigars would be smoked at sporting events. But his 'Superlative Cigar' and 'Royal Smoke' were always Havanas.

He described the 'Royal Smoke' thus, 'It is the King of cigars – the cigar you take to the banquet at which you know there will be speeches. But it is at one of those affairs to which you are compelled to go, and at which a series of dreary speeches are likely to follow one another, that the super-cigar really comes into its own. There you sit looking important, wise, content and apparently drinking in every word of each speaker. Actually, your astral body has been wafted far away by the delicate aroma, by the soul-satisfying flavour, by the mellow sweetness of the pluperfect stick of ripe tobacco leaf.'

Passion for Cuban leaf

This romantic tribute is one example of hundreds that litter the world of cigar writing. But it demonstrates the intertwined romance of the Havana cigar, a sense of occasion and an upper-class lifestyle.

Love for the Cuban leaf continues through the present day even though the superiority of the Havana cigar is no longer clear. Nevertheless it is the Cuban soil and Cuban brands which reach deepest into the passionado's imagination. The history and tradition exemplified by humble farmers in Pinar del Rio and *torcedors* in bustling Havana connect today's enthusiasts to their counterparts from centuries past.

Well over one hundred different cigars are produced in Cuba every year and not all of them are profiled here, only the very best produced. It is useful to listen to the opinions of trusted fellow smokers who have tried different cigars to find out about other cigars that have not been included here.

Cohiba

Habanos S.A.

Tel: +537 204 0524, www.habanos.com

There is no more exclusive cigar brand in the world than Cohiba. Its iconic yellow and black art deco style is recognisable to anyone with an interest in the good life.

Its lineage is remarkably short. The brand began life when Fidel Castro noticed that one of his bodyguards always smoked deliciously aromatic cigars. Fidel smoked some of these cigars and almost immediately he set up the cigar maker as his personal *torcedor*. This was the birth of Cohiba.

Miami cigar community

In the 1950s, Havana was the capital of cigars, but after the Revolution, most of the industry scattered. Finally another capital clearly emerged in Miami, in the expatriate Cuban cigar enthusiasts.

Cigar factories around the Caribbean Sea export most of their production to the US; and nearly all of it flows through Miami. Because of this, most non-Cuban cigar companies made their bases in Miami, often the neighbourhood of Little Havana.

Today, this mix of Cubans and cigar companies has brought Miami a vibrant cigar culture and is the best place in the US to smoke cigars, find small brands and discover boutique cigar factories.

To open a factory for the creation of Cohiba cigars, Fidel enlisted his trusted guerilla commander Celia Sanchez. In 1966 she transformed a colonial villa with vast gardens in the Laguito, Little Lake neighbourhood on the outskirts of Havana. The factory came to be known as El Laguito.

An ovular driveway circles from Avenida 146 up to the grand steps of El Laguito and then back past a guard shack down to the street. The driveway is no longer in use but the vast lawn that it encircles adds drama to the factory's entrance. The building is only two stories tall and additional facilities have been added behind it and on a neighbouring property to accommodate production and administrative requirements.

On the ground floor are two 'L'-shaped rolling galleries where employees work away in yellow uniforms making the Cohibas most demanded at the moment. Between the galleries is a grand circular staircase and a platform where the lector sits. The lector reads newspapers and novels into a microphone which amplifies his voice around the decaying but grand building.

To ascend the stairs is to enter the most secured portion of the building. This is where finished cigars are checked for quality and sorted by colour. Once sorted, the cigars are sent to another room where bands are added and the cigars are placed in either aluminium tubes or cedar boxes.

The expansion of the factory was largely due to the introduction of a second line of Cohibas in 1492.

Words from the wise

Hamlet Jaime Paredas
Cigar roller, Habanos, Cuba

» How to roll the perfect cigar

To get a perfect draw on a cigar, one of the best styles of rolling a cigar is known as *entubado*. I roll each tobacco leaf into a little tube before it goes in the bunch, so that each one looks like a little straw. First I make a row of tubes from Volado and Seco leaves. Then I lay the Ligero leaf on top and wrap the Volado and Seco around the Ligero. This puts the Ligero in the centre of the cigar and makes it burn perfectly.

Not all rollers roll like this. Many people fold the leaves together, but when this is done incorrectly, it can burn imperfectly, which will harm the cigar's taste. Sometimes the bad draw is due to applying the binder unevenly. When a roller uses a binder that is too short for the cigar, they need to patch in a second piece. The problem is when they use leaves in different angles which makes a tight spot in the bunch. But when you roll *entubado* and keep the binder at a constant angle, you get a great cigar.

Classics

The first Cohibas to be made were all together called Classics, Linea Classica in Spanish. This line was released in 1989 as an official brand though some sizes had been made earlier. The Linea Classica includes the Esplendido, Especiales, Exquisito, Panetela and Robusto. Two of these stand out from the crowd.

» Esplendido

Le Snob ESSENTIAL When Cohiba became commercially available in 1989, the Churchill *vitola* became an instant classic. It is big and bold, yet complex and refined. Its tastes and essences are many and for many smokers it defines the taste of tobacco. The Esplendido is in fact, splendid.

» Lancero

Lanceros are long, slim and elegant. No other *vitola* is known to showcase the taste of the wrapper leaf like the Lancero. The Cohiba Lancero pairs Cuba's best-graded tobacco wrapper and a *vitola* that shows it off. This makes the cigar spectacular. Its smoking characteristics are enough to merit high marks but this cigar also has a special connection to the history of the brand.

The Lancero is the *vitola* that Fidel's bodyguard smoked and it was therefore the inspiration for the entire Cohiba brand. In fact, Fidel was so enamoured with the cigar that it was the Cohiba Lancero which was Cuba's primary diplomatic gift during the early years of the Castro government.

1492 Siglos

In 1992 the Linea 1492 was added to the regular offerings from Cohiba. The original introductions were the Siglo I, Siglo II, Siglo III, Siglo IV and Siglo V. They were made to highlight another taste profile that can be created with Cuba's top-quality tobacco.

The collection ranges in taste from the punchy little Siglo I to the smooth and rich Siglo VI. Siglo means century in Spanish and each *vitola* commemorated a century since Christopher visited Cuba. In 2002, Habanos broke the mould and released a sixth siglo (Siglo VI) about ninety years early. Very few complain as this is one of the most desired Habanos today.

» **Siglo I**

This cigar introduces itself like it has something to prove. It measures only four inches by forty ring gauge but vastly outperforms expectations. People may expect pleasant floral, cereal and tobacco tastes from a Perla-sized Cohiba. What it delivers is a full-flavoured, spicy, rich concoction of top-quality tobacco. Almost no cigar goes so perfectly with strong coffee in the middle of the day.

Siglo IV selection

Le Snob ESSENTIAL When most people think of the Siglo taste, they imagine the taste they get from the number Four. Perhaps this is because it is neatly situated in the middle range of ring gauges and lengths. Or perhaps it is because the Siglo IV just seems perfect. Its balance almost disguises its complexity. The tastes of toasted cereals, nuts, light spices, pepper and floral aromas all exist in this 46-ring gauge corona gorda.

UNIQUE » RARE » LITTLE-KNOWN » ULTIMATE **Snob**

Monsdales at Club Havana Before the Cuban Revolution, Club Havana was a private beach club. Fewer people frequent the club today – Club Havana is now for cigar lovers.

In the back of the club is a cigar store called La Casa del Habano, run by a tobacco expert, Enrique Mons, who has cigars custom made for his clientele. He knows everything about the tobacco leaf. An afternoon discussing cigars with him is akin to an undergraduate degree in cigars.

For the sublimest of pleasures, ask about the cigar that bears his name; he has created a blend of tobaccos that harmoniously combine to showcase their best flavours. Rolled into his favourite shape, the Lonsdale, it is called the 'Monsdale,' and it is a rite of passage to come here and smoke one.

» Siglo VI

James Suckling, a cigar journalist, has had a tremendous impact on the popularity of this cigar with his rating of 100/100. The fat ring gauge, 52, allows lots of tobacco to be rolled into the Siglo VI. Despite all this tobacco, the Six's taste is more mellow than the previously mentioned One and Four. What the Six delivers in spades is a long, cool smoke with lots of refined flavours.

Cohiba innovations

Recent years have produced more innovation in the Cuban cigar industry than at any time in history. The brand that has given its name to more offspring than any other is Cohiba. In 2008, Cuba could no longer ignore the global demand for a Maduro wrapped cigar. So with the full force of their most exclusive brand, Habanos released the Cohiba Maduro 5.

» Cohiba Maduro 5

Limited Edition Habanos had borne Maduro leaves since 2000. But no suitable cigar had been created which could wear the maduro coat full-time. Timidly, Habanos released the Maduro 5 in three sizes called the Magicos, Genios and Magnificos. Most notably the cigars exhibit an aroma of old leather and sweet woodiness. Their taste is highly refined. Different from other Cohiba lines, these dark cigars have a slightly sweet, dark flavour.

Behike

Nearly every global cigar brand has a full-flavoured father figure. A cigar with largess and dominance over the rest of their offerings. Cuba did not have a 'big daddy'. The flagship cigar, the Cohiba Esplendido, was highly refined with excellent balance and modest strength.

In 2010 this all changed. Cohiba's Behike BHK 52, 54 and 56 were released to the market with incredible flair. The cigars are big in every way. Ring gauges are denoted by the names and range from 52 to the monstrous 56. But size was not enough. Habanos put a special ingredient into the Behike BHK which made it the strongest Habano on the market.

040

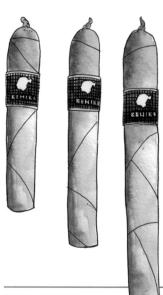

« **Cohiba Behike,** claimed to be 'the most exclusive *línea* of the most prestigious Habanos brand'.

The ingredient is the Medio Tiempo leaf. This leaf grows at the very top of the plant, in the *corona* or crown. Sitting at the top, the leaf gathers tremendous amounts of sunshine and develops into a thick, coarse and über-flavourful leaf. For decades, this leaf was considered too strong for exported brands. But smoker's tastes have changed and Habanos reacted.

» **BHK 52**

The 52 has half a leaf of Medio Tiempo, which gives the engorged Robusto a tremendous kick. The base blend is quite modest so the Medio Tiempo shines with its strong spice.

» **BHK 54**

Half a leaf of Medio Tiempo is also used in the BHK 54 despite its larger ring gauge. The 54 is the weakest of the three Behike BHKs but it is no powder puff. It is the cigar, of the three, that most showcases the non-Medio Tiempo flavours of the blend.

» **BHK 56**

Le Snob ESSENTIAL A full leaf of Medio Tiempo, a massive ring gauge and long length give this cigar a striking presence. In has been called the 'Billionaire's Cigar' because it seems like the type of cigar you would find at Davos or on a private island. It is the strongest of the three and is the Havana cigar which will stand up to the strongest drink pairings after the richest meals.

Cohiba finest

Not all of Cohiba's innovation has followed global trends. In 2009, Habanos returned to a classic formula. The formula is to take the highest-quality leaf, ferment it until all that is left is pure, rich, tobacco flavour. What they created was the Cohiba Grand Reserva. This cigar was only a limited release but it demonstrated to purists that the historic company had not lost contact with its roots.

» Cohiba Grand Reserva

Le Snob ESSENTIAL The cigar, crafted at El Laguito, demonstrates all the best qualities of Cuban craftsmanship from the field to the rolling gallery. All the leaves used to make the blend were aged for a minimum of five years and the wrapper was aged for seven. Only the most flavourful and flawless-looking leaves were used. It is a richer version of the famed Siglo VI. Its taste elevates the already great Siglo VI profile by adding sweetness and bolder woody notes. The result of which was one of the finest cigars ever produced anywhere, ever.

Partagas

Habanos S.A., for information see page 33

Havana's most prominent and visited factory is Partagas. It sits next to Central Park and in the shadow of the country's formerly glorious Capitol building. It is an historic brand with roots reaching deep into the nineteenth century.

Don Jaime Partagas was a Spaniard who moved to Cuba in the early nineteenth century. By 1845, his cigars must have been very popular because he upgraded facilities and built the monstrous building we know today as the Partagas Factory. The company was sold to Jose Bance, then Ramon Cifuentes Llano and his business partners. The Cifuentes family became the sole owners of the brand and factory just two decades before the revolution. At that date, of course, the Cuban State took over operations and finances at the company.

Partagas is known in the Habanos portfolio as the spicy one. Its bright, red bands signify to smokers – this is a strong cigar, proceed with caution. It is precisely this character that draws enthusiasts to the brand in large numbers and has for nearly 200 years.

The brand can be found with two distinct bands. One band is bright red with bold gold letters and horizontal gold lines. This band dresses the lettered lines: A, B, C, D and P. The other band is the classically ornate Cifuentes y Cia band.

» Signs of age

Cuban cigars are the easiest to date, as since 1985 the
bottoms of the boxes have been stamped with a boxing
date. Older Cuban cigars are more challenging but
many clues can be gleaned from tax stamps and
modifications in packaging over the years. The Cuban
warranty seal, featured on every box, was printed from
the same plates from 1931 to 1998. As time passed, the
plates wore down and the details became fuzzy. The
right side of the seal features an image of farmers in a
tobacco field, which appear clearly in the earliest
prints, but towards the end of the century, only three
workers could be clearly identified.

Dating non-Cuban cigars is extraordinarily difficult
because no manufacturer has consistently marked
their boxes. You can try a web search – labels and
boxes change over time and any slight change can be a
clue. Otherwise, call the manufacturer. Nobody
recalls slight package changes better than the makers.

>> **Serie D. No. 4**

Most popular among the lettered cigars is the Partagas Serie D #4. It is 123mm long with a ring gauge of 50, a size well known as Robusto. This particular Partagas has been made since the 1930s with only minimal adjustments to the size and blend.

Both the brand Partagas, and the size Robusto, imply big flavour. And for many years, this cigar has not disappointed. In the past, this cigar would have been a Le Snob Essential but recent years productions have not lived up to the legacy. From 2005–2010, these cigars have been produced with mixed results. The great ones still exist but there are also many boxes which require several years of aging to mature into the cigars they are supposed to be.

>> **Serie D. No. 1**

Le Snob ESSENTIAL Lettered series Partagas cigars have largely been discontinued. Since 2004, quite a few have reemerged as Limited Editions. While all have been of excellent quality, one stands out from the pack. The Serie D. No. 1 was once discontinued. In 2004 it was re-blended and re-released just for that year. The *vitola* just a bit shorter than a Churchill came out with a beautiful colourado-Maduro wrapper.

As these cigars have aged, they have reached legendary status. The combination of Partagas' rich blend and the thick, sweet, Maduro wrapper leaf have matured remarkably over time. Strong oaky aromas, light complex spice and deep, dark sweetness now characterise the cigar.

Cifuentes y Cia, Partagas

>> Lusitania

Very similar to a Churchill, the Partagas Lusitania is 7¼" long with a 50 ring gauge. It is long, noble and noticeable. It is perhaps the most iconic of the Partagas *vitolas* and features a tapered then rounded head.

Its fame is partly due to the way that the *vitola* harnesses the spice of the Partagas character and delivers it in concert with earthiness. The combination brings forth an enviable complexity and refinement not found in many strong cigars. With age, this cigar grows in breadth of flavour. Floral aromas begin to succeed to the fore demonstrating the world-class blending behind this particular cigar.

>> Partagas Short

A delicious display of complex and powerful flavours are displayed in the 42 ring gauge by 110mm Partagas Short. It is not terribly strong, perhaps due to length, but it delivers flavour by the barrow.

This smoke is notable not only for its supreme elegance in youth but more so for its massive flavour with age. This cigar changes its flavour profile somewhat dramatically as it ages. What starts out as an earthy and spicy little smoke, becomes a tremendously aromatic floral cigar with a few years of age. It is one of the few cigars that continues to produce flavour in large doses as it ages.

Montecristo

Habanos S.A., for information see page 33

Habanos S.A., for information see page 33

More Montecristo cigars are purchased than any other Habanos cigar. It is a brand that captures the essence of Cuban tobacco. It wears an understated brown band but a grand name that reaches into literary regency.

Its deep, woody and rich flavours remind the smoker of the country's legacy as a producer of strong cigars. Even the brown band seems to suggest its flavour.

Among its icons are the simply named Number 2, Number 4 and A. Simple *vitola* names have lasted centuries because one need only say 'Montecristo' to evoke the character of these rich, woody, very Cuban cigars. It is their excellent balance and medium-bodied character that make these cigars so popular. Anyone from novice to expert will find that Montecristo cigars fit in their smoking calendar at some time.

» Montecristo #2

Le Snob
ESSENTIAL

Montecristo #2 is the most known Torpedo-shaped cigar in the world. It is an icon and it represents the Montecristo brand well. Its flavours are rich, with medium earthy, cereal, sweet, lightly spiced tastes. It may be the cigar that most represents a meal.

Its dimensions have become the standard for all Torpedoes at 156mm and 52 ring gauge. In many ways, this cigar represents the middle ground of the best Cuban cigars. Its flavours are classically Cuban while not too strong and not too mild. It has less spice than Partagas and more earth than a brand like H. Upmann. The 'Monte #2' as it is styled, has earned its place as an iconic cigar over half a century.

Jazz and cigars in Havana

One of the only expressions of pre-revolution Havana alive today is its connection with live jazz. While there are numerous places to enjoy live music, three stand out as regular sites for top-quality music. All are cigar-friendly.

El Gato Tuerto (The One-Eyed Cat) is a high-energy music and dance club located in a ritzy townhouse one block from the Hotel Nacional. It features music every evening.

La Zorra y El Cuervo (The Fox and the Crow) is marked by an English-style phone booth at its entrance. The music is among the best in the city. There is no dancing but its mood is very chilled out.

La Casa de Musica (The House of Music) has two locations; one in Havana and one in Miramar. Both are centres for the best Cuban performers.

>> Montecristo #4

The best-selling cigar of all Habanos, is the Montecristo #4. It is a Mareva (129mm by 42 ring gauge), which gives it enough heft to be smoked late in the day and the short length required by after-lunch smokers.

Like other Montecristos, the taste is earthy, savoury and of cereals, mushrooms and light sweetness. Its popularity is due to the versatility of its size but also to the palatability of its flavours. With coffee or Armagnac, the Montecristo #4 is very often the right choice for the moment.

>> Montecristo 'A'

Of all the large cigars, none have the staying power of the Montecristo A. It has existed since at least the 1970s and has survived while many other large cigars have disappeared. Again, it is probably the medium, earthy flavours which have kept this cigar in production. Few people find the time, up to three hours, to smoke such a grand cigar but when they do, they reach for a Montecristo A.

Hoyo de Monterrey

Habanos S.A., for information see page 33

Named for a hole in the earth in which excellent tobacco is grown, Hoyo de Monterrey are some of the most glamorous Cuban cigars. The cigars are blended to the middle of the flavour range but are less dark than Montecristo. Their taste is characterised as more creamy and aromatic with a nutty finish.

UNIQUE » RARE » LITTLE-KNOWN » ULTIMATE **Snob**

Lanesborough Hotel Few cigar vendors offer the opportunity to sample the rarest cigars, as they can't afford to carry the stock. London's Lanesborough Hotel is the exception to this rule.

Giuseppe Ruo manages the Garden Room, which is an outdoor space dedicated to the enjoyment of fine cigars and libations. The humidor is extremely well stocked, only the best premium cigars are available. Among rarities recently available, the Cohiba Behike stands above the rest.

With a price tag of $2,500, this cigar is not for everyone but for the rare cigar enthusiast, the Lanesborough makes those cigars available. The humidor also features Edicion Limitada Cuban cigars and some modest regular production smokes – but only those hand selected by Giuseppe.

» **Epicure Especial**

A new addition to the Hoyo de Monterrey line, this larger version of the Epicure cigars (Epicure #1 & #2) delivers pure bliss. It is less subtle than some of the softer Hoyos. Right from the light, the Epicure Especial brings an earthy component to the creamy character of the brand. It delivers light flavours of wood, mushroom and herbs and is suitable to smoke after dinner despite its lightness.

» **Double Corona**

Le Snob ESSENTIAL Hoyo's flagship is the Double Corona. These were considered the best cigar during the cigar boom of the late 1990s and were nearly impossible to find. They epitomise the brand's smooth character. This cigar is loved by the seasoned smoker who appreciates the subtle complexity of Cuban tobacco. WIth age, the cigars mature and their aroma develops into something entirely unique. For the patient enthusiast, the Hoyo de Monterrey is a treasure, to be visited every few months as it matures.

Minor and rare brands

Some cigars are sold in small quantities. Others are no longer sold at all. These are the cigars that are only found in the humidors of the knowledgeable enthusiast. Each one has a story to tell, and it is a story you may not have heard before.

» Davidoff Cuban Cigars

Davidoff Cuban Cigars were made in the El Laguito factory from 1969 to 1992. These cigars were considered the best of the best, or at least to have very few competitors in the space. Now it is rare to find Davidoff cigars marked with 'CUBA' on the band. Those that can be found carry a high price tag and many have passed their peak taste. Because so many of these have passed their peak, it is not advisable to buy them without proof of provenance and some suggestion that they are yet smokeable.

» Dunhill Cuban Cigars

Another brand of cigars no longer made in Cuba is Dunhill. They were made from 1984 to 1991 and were considered to be on par with Davidoff. Because these cigars were made in much smaller quantities than Davidoff, their prices have skyrocketed in recent years. The same guidance as with Davidoff can be offered as regards purchasing these cigars.

» Juan Lopez

Today, Juan Lopez cigars are produced in very small quantities. They have a noticeably woody character and are light in flavour overall. What makes these cigars noteworthy is their aging potential. Juan Lopez cigars are remarkably well and develop excellent complexity over time without losing flavour. This is exactly the type of cigar that Le Snob holds in stock because it ages better than most and carries the torch for small brands with distinct and attractive flavours.

» Ramon Allones

Small production, exuberant lithography and rich taste characterise the Ramon Allones brand. These cigars have not been widely popular among cigar smokers because the taste is not classic. It brings together disperate tastes to create something quite unique. Despite low production, this is a brand steeped in history. Ramon Allones was a pioneer in the use of colour lithography for cigar boxes and bands. The legacy can be seen today on bright green boxes.

The Ramon Allones Robusto (124 mm by 50 ring gauge) is awkwardly called the Specially Selected. But when you get past the name, the cigar delivers excellent flavour. It is medium to strong and delivers both high notes of natural sweetness and dark notes of wood. Its balance can be dubious while young but with a few years' age, it typically becomes sensuous. This is another cigar that the connoisseur cherishes and keeps on hand, revisiting every few months to check its progress.

» Honduras

Development of an industry

Honduras was a tobacco-producing country even before the Cuban Revolution. But as with all countries now producing premium cigars, the exodus from Cuba, caused by the revolution, was like rocket fuel for their cigar production.

In the late fifties and early sixties, Frank Llaneza, Oliva Tobacco, and the Cuban Land and Leaf Tobacco Company all began planting Cuban seeds in Honduras. They would become pioneers in a movement that ultimately overtook Cuba in the production of premium cigars.

Premium soil

Honduras was chosen for its rich soil. The Jamastran valley resembled parts of Pinar del Rio that growers knew to be excellent for tobacco, so some of the first plantings were made there. With time, areas like Copan in the north and Trojes in the south-east were added to the primary locations of excellent tobacco in the country.

Unique flavours

What distinguishes Honduran tobacco from others is its rich, earthy taste. Tim Ozgener, President of CAO cigars, relates that he loves to use Ligero leaf from Jamastran. The earthy taste it provides is like nothing found elsewhere. His cigars La Traviata and Criollo, with their earthy flavours, doubtlessly use handfuls of Honduran leaf.

Expansion in Honduras

During the years of US embargo against Nicaragua, many cigar makers shifted their production up the pan-American highway into Danli, Honduras. Some producers, such as Padron Cigars, moved back to Nicaragua at the end of the troubles. But many remained in Danli. Honduras was the powerhouse that proved on a large scale that Central American cigars were world class.

Punch

Swedish Match Company, USA

Tel: +1(804) 302 1700, www.cigarworld.com

The Punch brand began in Cuba under the famed manufacturer Manuel Lopez. In 1840, when he created the brand, he named it for the popular creature from the Punch and Judy comedies. The marketing worked and the brand thrived, especially in the United Kingdom, for over a decade. At the time of the Cuban Revolution, Villazon began making the cigar under Frank Llaneza in Honduras.

Ultimately, the cigar took on a largely Central American blend and a strong character, not unlike the Punch character from comics. What is notable in this line is its extremely high quality and low price.

» **Punch After Dinner Maduro**

 This dark, elegant cigar has exemplified Central American finesse for decades. It delivers a powerful taste and dark aroma that is essentially earthy and woody. But it is made harmonious with sweet notes and light spice. It is a smooth smoke but it requires short aging time. This cigar should not be smoked upon purchase. It should be allowed to mellow for eight to fourteen months. After that point, the cigar is world class. At its low price, it is worth the wait.

Don Rolando Reyes

114 NW 22nd Avenue, Miami, FL 33125

Tel: +1(800) 992 4427

Rolando Reyes was the factory manager at a Cuban cigar factory called Cuba Aliados. When the independent cigar factory was finally shut down, Rolando was given the legal ownership of the name Cuba Aliados as thanks for his years of work.

In 1972, Rolando moved away from Cuba and ultimately ended up in Honduras making cigars again. Despite being a factory worker in Cuba, in Honduras he is a man of the land. He grows his own produce and meat on one and a half mountains that he owns. His factory sits on the property and every afternoon, Rolando makes his way to the factory to check on the day's production. Today, his most popular cigars include the Cienfuegos and Puros Indios.

» Cienfuegos

Cienfuegos is a full-strength, hot and spicy cigar with Nicaraguan and Dominican tobaccos. This is the company's boldest offering at the moment.

» Puros Indios

For a brand that is as popular as it is, Puros Indios is not very often spoken about. Perhaps its curse is that it is a known commodity and is still in such regular demand that it need not make waves. The cigars have a delicate flavour of sweetness and spice.

UNIQUE » RARE » LITTLE-KNOWN » ULTIMATE **Snob**

Centenary cigars One-hundred-year-old cigars are rare; smokeable ones are even rarer. In 2008, three boxes of cigars from the late 19th century were found in Oxfordshire, England. They had been in the wine cellar of a manor house for over a century. Because the cellar was consistently moist and cool throughout the years, the cigars were preserved in smokeable condition.

I was able to taste some of the 130-year-old H. Upmann and Cabanas cigars. The wrappers were delicate and prone to cracking but the tobacco kept its nutty, floral and spiced tastes and aromas.

This was an important find, demonstrating that cigars of this age can be tasty. In the past, ultra-aged cigars were primarily collected as artifacts, not for smoking. Many collectors devalued them, despite their rarity, because of poor taste expectations. Collectors responded quickly and now consider these cigars more investible. They now achieve higher prices at auction.

Camacho

4650 NW 74th Avenue, Miami, Florida 33166

Tel: +1(305) 592 0722, www.camachocigars.com

Julio and Christian Eiroa are the father and son, respectively, team who have run Caribe Imported Cigars. Julio left Cuba with his mother and brothers after the communist policies of the Cuban Revolution were felt in their home of Pinar del Rio. He returned briefly as part of the Bay of Pigs military operation but returned to Miami and Honduras to work in Tobacco.

Over thirty years, Julio created a business that made and sold over two million cigars per year. The best selling among them were Baccarat and La Fontana. Baccarat is still the company's biggest-selling cigar. In 1995, the Eiroas bought the Camacho brand and began to create an entirely different style of cigar. Whereas their Baccarat is smooth and mild, Camacho cigars are quite the opposite. Some cigars stand out from the lines.

» Camacho Diploma Scorpion

Le Snob
ESSENTIAL
In the Corojo area of Pinar del Rio, the Eiroa family dealt with the benefits and shortcomings of the Corojo leaf. When they left Cuba they took the seed with them and have spent all their time in Honduras cultivating and improving the seed. It has been their primary seed type for decades and many of their cigars feature at least some of the Honduran Corojo leaf.

The Camacho Diploma Scorpion, is filled with Honduran Corojo. This full-bodied cigar really

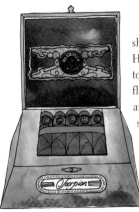

showcases the richness of Honduran tobacco. It is blended to be complex while showcasing flavours on the woody, spiced and savoury side of the flavour spectrum. It is better fermented than many of the Camacho cigars, which allows the rich tobacco flavour to be unmasked as soon as you remove it from the box.

It is only released occasionally and in small quantities. Adding to its allure further, the cigar is tapered at both ends. It bulges to 60 ring gauge in the middle but is quite manageable at the ends.

» Triple Maduro

During the late two-thousands, the demand for Maduro wrapped cigars grew to a crescendo. Manufacturers used all kinds of leaves to create Maduro wrappers. Cusano even used two Maduro wrappers to dress a cigar. As if to end the debate, Camacho released a cigar called the Triple Maduro.

It is so named because the wrapper, binder and filler are all considered Maduro by Camacho. Since Maduro simply means aged, the tobacco that goes into this cigar is aged before it is rolled. In order to age well without disintigrating, a manufacturer has to use thick leaves. Therefore the Camacho Triple Maduro is a big, smooth-tasting (because of the age) dark beauty. It feels heavy and lumpy in the hand but it is interesting as a concept and, most importantly, it is very tasty.

» Who is the lector?

Torcedors today listen to headphones or piped-in music. This was not always the case. During most of the 20th century, cigar rollers listened to the voice of a lector who read the daily newspaper and novels. Each factory would make space for a lector somewhere on the production floor. Often, as in the H. Upmann factory, they would be elevated above the rollers, at a table, so that they could be heard above the sounds of the *chavetas*.

Whether they would read novels or the daily newspaper depended upon the preferences of the rollers, who would hold a vote. The rollers controlled the reading by paying the lector themselves, cutting the factory owner out of the arrangement.

Today, very few factories still employ a lector. Notably, the ones that do include the Puros Indios factory in Honduras, H. Upmann and El Laguito in Havana, and La Aurora in the Dominican Republic.

Torano

Tel: +1(305) 661 9121, www.torano.com

Few cigar-maker families have the pedigree that the Toranos do. Since 1912, they have been in the tobacco business first in Cuba, as leaf brokers then farmers, and now as cigar makers under their Torano brand. Their best cigars exist in the Exodus lines of cigars they make. They explain that the brand is called 'Exodus' to recall their undesired departure from Cuba when tobacco farms were nationalised.

≫ Exodus 1959 – 50 Years

The copper-banded Exodus is called the 50 Years because it came out fifty years after the family felt forced to leave Cuba. Regardless of its name, the cigar is spectacular. It is a blend of tobaccos from around the world and has a Honduran binder. Its taste is rich and bold but also rounded and smooth. The complexity of flavours is notable for its spicy, sweetness and savoury notes.

≫ Exodus 1959 Silver Edition

The Silver Edition has been with us for many years and has earned its place in the humidor as an exquisitely crafted cigar with wonderful medium flavours. It has a lovely complexity that binds flavours of acidic fruit and light earthy flavours.

Rocky Patel

Tel: +1(239) 593 1833, www.rockypatel.com

The Rocky Patel Premium Cigar Company is based in Florida, but buys in materials and rents factory space from Nestor Plasencia (see page 93), in both Honduras and Nicaragua. For fifteen years, Rocky Patel has impressed the cigar world with excellent cigar after excellent cigar. Unfortunately, during this same period, his cigars have not always been consistent. He has struggled with this and striven to rectify the problem. If the past few years are any indication, it looks like he has rounded the corner on this issue and the cigars that came out to such acclaim will remain as good as the first examples.

>> **Decade**

The Decade cigar was released to celebrate Rocky Patel's tenth year in the premium cigar business. He wanted to create something timeless, and he succeeded. The cigar is characterised by excellent balance. It combines woody, savoury and lightly spicy flavours to create a cigar that will fit in nearly any situation. It goes just as well with coffee as it does with fine cognac.

>> **Decade Edicion Limitada**

Le Snob ESSENTIAL This is a Maduro-wrapped version of the popular Decade cigar. But the transformation that this wrapper causes is incredible. It brings the already spectacular Decade cigar into the rarified air in which only the world's best cigars burn. The Maduro leaf adds rich cocoa sweetness to the already savoury and tasty blend described above.

Raices Cubanas

www.illusionecigars.com

The historic factories have produced their excellent sticks for years or even generations. But Honduras is pulsing with innovative takes on premium tobacco. The factory at the heart of this is called Raices Cubanas. It houses top-quality rollers and tobacco largely from Tabacalera Tropical. Some of the innovators producing cigars there include Dion Giolito, Alan Rubin and Charlie Torano.

Illusione

Dion Giolito seemed an unlikely brand owner when he first appeared on the scene. His style is Punk Rock and his sideburns extend nearly to his lips. But from Reno, Nevada, this cigar-store owner created a cigar brand that is among the best in the world with Illusione.

» Illusione 888 Slam

Dion's incredibly popular Illusione line has many stars. The HL has won awards but the fatter *vitolas* are the most popular cigars for daily smoking. One among the fatter cigars can possibly both win awards and satisfy the connoisseur after a steak dinner. This is the Illusione 888 Slam.

The Slam is a bench-pressed version of the round 888. During the cigar's production, the 888 is made in the traditional way but then it is placed in a square mould after the wrapper has been applied. It is squished into a rectangular and more compact shape which modifies the taste. The compactness and the

Words from the wise

Craig Schneider Columnist for
cigarmedia.tv, USA

» Retrohaling

Retrohaling, or expelling smoke from the mouth out
the nose without inhaling it, adds value to cigar
smoking. The smoker breathes out through the nose
while the mouth is full of smoke, and the smoke
then wisps out from the nose.

The technique can reveal a huge range of flavours
contained within the smoke that are not perceivable
with normal smoking and tasting when the smoke is
just drawn into the mouth, and allows you to sense
different intensities of the flavours already tasted.
The breadth of flavours are easier to perceive in the
nose – the taste of sweetness in the mouth may
become defined as caramel or light sugar when the
smoke is passed through the nose.

Retrohaling can cause irritation of the nose but
usually only with improperly processed tobacco or if
too much smoke is passed through the nose.

different contact of the tobaccos causes the cigar to taste differently, and in the case of this cigar – the result is spectacular.

» Illusione HL (Holy Lance)

Le Snob ESSENTIAL The Lancero in Dion's Illusione line-up is called the Holy Lance or HL for short. Despite its strange name, it is an extraordinary example of Central American tobacco. Small ring gauge cigars best showcase the flavour of their wrappers. They are not dominated by *ligero* and the wrapper makes up a large percentage of the total tobacco. Dion uses this to the advantage of the HL.

It is a long, elegant, rich and flavourful Lancero. The dark wrapper is not rustic. Somehow the wrapper is dark and thick, masculine and elegant. Its flavours range dramatically within the parameters of savoury, woody, sweet, floral and spicy tastes and aromas.

Alec Bradley

Tel: +1(888) 426 4397, www.alecbradley.com

Alan Rubin named his sons, and then named his cigar company after the boys, Alec and Bradley. Today the brand is one of the fastest growing in the US. On the back of high ratings, Alan has moved in front of the headlights of the US cigar consumer. His recent cigars are very interesting because they are from the new school of cigar taste. The Tempus cigar is a good example of this school which features

From Nicaragua to Honduras

The distance between Esteli, Nicaragua and Danli, Honduras, Central America's cigar capitals, is not far. Cigar makers travel back and forth to buy tobacco every week. Despite physical closeness, the distance seems long because of the mountains and heavily policed border. In order to protect against trade in illegal goods, both countries tightly restrict the crossing.

Most buses terminate at the border. This means that a traveller needs to leave the bus, walk across the border and find a new bus on the other side. Of late, even taxis are prevented from crossing unless they have permission from both countries. Using buses, especially in Honduras, is considered dangerous for visitors. The best way to make this crossing is in a private car with a driver.

big, easy tastes that do not change from beginning to end, hallmarks of the style.

›› Tempus

As described before, the Tempus cigar is part of the new school of cigar blending. In the case of this particular cigar, the flavour is like a savoury chocolate sundae. It has a dark chocolate bitterness, some rich savoury caramel tastes and nuttiness as if peanuts were sprinkled across the sundae. The flavour remains perfectly consistent from lighting to putting the cigar down.

Jesus Fuego

Tabacos S.A., 10401 NW 28th St # B-101, Miami, Florida 33172

In any profession there exist those who obtain attention, and those who diligently toil under the radar and create products at least as good as those made by the headline grabbers. In the world of cigars, Jesus Fuego is a man working hard and creating tremendous cigars. Uniquely, Jesus actually studied the science of tobacco fermentation during his university and masters degree programs. He is an expert and now has the delicious cigars to prove it.

›› Origen

Le Snob ESSENTIAL The cigar line Origen is a family affair. The wrapper, from Brazil, is grown by Jesus' father Jose. The binder and filler are selected especially to create this hearty, rich and sweetly balanced cigar. The most unique cigar in the line is called the Original.

At five inches and a forty-four ring gauge in the middle, the Original is a truly original cigar. Well, it is unique to connoisseurs but not unique to *tabaqueros*. The cigar is made without moulds, entirely by hand. Therefore the shape varies a little bit from cigar to cigar. It is short and skinny with a bulge in the middle, much like the popular cigars of the nineteenth century. What astounds is the powerful flavour and extreme refinement of the blend brought out by perfect fermentation and tobacco matching. For those rare moments where a strange little Perfecto is required, a cigar aficionado must have this on hand. The Original is like a passport on to the tobacco farm.

Gurkha

Tel: +1(305) 593 2254, www.gurkhacigars.com

Gurkha cigars are some of the most exclusive in the world. Many are made in the Danli factory now owned by Scandanavian Tobacco and operated by the Olivas family. While the cigars are excellent, many people know the brand for its spectacular, often hand-crafted boxes. Gurkha boxes range from brass nailed wooden chests to ultra-refined leather cases.

» Gurkha Triad Platinum

Most people know this cigar because of its price and haven't bothered to smoke it. It is well worth smoking. The Triad utilises tobacco from some of the most exotic locations around the world, including Sub-Saharan Africa. The taste is spectacularly complex with a tanginess that is not found in any other cigar to date.

» Maya Selva

Franco-Honduran Maya Selva is an icon among Honduran cigar makers. Her grace and style is not only visible but it is rolled into her cigars. One of her masterpieces is the Flor de Selva Churchill. It is a cigar supremely balanced with aromas of cedar, herbs, white pepper and light citrus sweetness.

» Nicaragua

Rising production

Nicaragua is the premier cigar country on the ascendent. Every year it is exporting more cigars than it did the year before. In 2010 it surpassed Honduras and became the second-largest producing country in the world.

Just a generation after revolution and economic embargo, Nicaraguan cigar makers are thriving. It is not just government policies that put Nicaragua in the express lane. Nicaraguan tobacco, which is famously strong and flavourful, features in the most popular cigars today. Established cigar makers are thriving and more makers are opening up shop every year.

Uniform among premium cigar producers in Nicaragua is high standard, big flavour cigars. This chapter highlights a small number of Nicaraguan producers who represent the best and most exciting cigars made in Nicaragua today. Some producers are passing the torch to younger generations. Others have only been in Nicaragua a handful of years. They are all top performers who score highly in magazine ratings.

Garcia Family

Tel: +1(305) 858 0001,
www.elreydeloshabanos.com

When cigar enthusiasts discuss the best cigar makers in the world, a short list emerges. One of the names firmly on that short list is Pepin (Jose) Garcia. The world's best tobacconists discuss his cigars with authority. They cite his many triumphs and his humble beginnings in rural Cuba. What is usually overlooked, is that Pepin only started his business in 2002!

He rose to the top of the industry in little time thanks to his devoted family and his extremely loyal clients. The brand he first introduced under his own name has become iconic: Don Pepin Garcia Blue Label.

» Don Pepin Garcia Blue Label

Blue bands rarely decorate premium cigars. But Pepin doesn't play by the rules and his Blue Label cigars epitomise his unique cigar blending style. The spicy, peppery taste that these cigars have are his signature. The taste seems to dance on the tongue and even evokes memories of Pepin's favourite drink – Scotch Whisky.

The Blue Label are made both in Nicaragua and Miami for different markets but the blend is the same. Wrapped with a Corojo leaf, the cigar's Nicaraguan fillers demonstrate the country's ability to produce strong and aromatic leaf.

» La Reloba

La Reloba is a brand made by Pepin that is not heavily marketed. It comes in two varieties, one with an Habano seed wrapper and the other with a wrapper of Sumatran seed. The Habano-wrapped cigar is rich and strong, containing lots of character and a nutty finish. The Sumatra version is highly refined, delivering creaminess, leathery aromas and subtle sweetness.

Among the many excellent cigars that Pepin makes under his own brands, La Reloba stands out as a top-quality cigar at a bargain price. It is made with all the flourishes of Cuban hand craftsmanship. Every cigar smoker likes to have big-named emblematic cigars in the humidor. But every cigar passionado makes sure to have lesser-known cigars of superior quality at the ready.

My Father, Le Bijou 1922

Jaime Garcia, Pepin's son, has invested his life and career in the family cigar business. He has a formal education in agronomy and has spent a good portion of his young life in tobacco fields and cigar factories. In 2008, Jaime brought out a cigar to honour his father called 'My Father'.

The cigar blend was created in Nicaragua by Jaime without his father's knowledge. It had to be made in Nicaragua because his secret would have been found out in the small Miami factory.

Originally the cigar was dressed in a Habano seed wrapper with a slightly reddish hue, called *rosado*. The blend is strong in flavour and is among the most complex cigars made by the family.

In 2009, a Maduro-wrapped version of My Father was released. It is a flavour bomb. The Maduro wrapper imparts a sweet, smooth, creaminess to the rich, spicy and intriguing underlying blend. In the tradition of honouring fathers, this version of the cigar is dedicated to Pepin's father and is called Le Bijou (The Jewel) 1922. The Churchill version of Le Bijou 1922 is one of the finest cigars available.

Tatuaje

www.tatuajecigars.com

When Pepin Garcia opened his first cigar factory in Miami FL, he relied upon the success of two companies in order to pay the rent. One was his own and the other was a start-up called Tatuaje, meaning Tatoo in English.

Tatuaje is the creation of Pete Johnson who was then a cigar buyer for the Grand Havana Room in Beverly Hills. He had long wanted to create a brand of cigars but could not find a cigar maker who would work with him the way he wanted. When Pepin went to Los Angeles as an event roller, he met Pete and they immediately went to work together.

Neither could speak the other's language but they both spoke tobacco. Pepin would create a blend. They would discuss it. Then Pepin would modify the blend and this continued for weeks. Pete shared some of his favourite Cuban cigars with Pepin and said, 'Can you make this?' Pepin, being very familiar with the Cuban blends, said, 'Sure, that will be easy, I know that one.'

Thus began a collaboration that continues today. Pete has expanded his portfolio to three lines of Tatuaje, Cabaiguan, La Verite, El Triunfador, La Riqueza and Ambos Mundos. Pepin makes all these cigars for Pete.

» Smoke and ice

Tobacco leaves have a cult following among humans
but are more popular among *Lasioderma Serricorne*,
the Tobacco Beetle. This beetle is found in all
tobacco-growing regions and once it reaches
maturity, it will eat all the tobacco it can find. Cigar
makers use two methods to ensure that the beetles
do not survive long enough to eat cigars. The two
most common methods are fumigation and freezing.

Fumigation leaves no lasting noticeable aroma or
taste, but it does eliminate the tobacco beetle and its
larvae before the cigars leave the country of
manufacture. Fumigation is typically performed on
completed cigars before exportation.

Freezing cigars is the other method used to remove
the beetle. The cigars are kept at low temperatures
for several days, within a factory's cold room, in
order to kill eggs, larvae and adult beetles before
they have the opportunity to eat any tobacco.

Tatuaje, La Seleccion de Cazador, Reserva SW

Le Snob ESSENTIAL The first line called Tatuaje is best known as the Brown Label. Its band is plain, with a brown background and white lettering which simply states, Tatuaje. The contrast between the graceful, proud lettering and the word itself is truly modern.

These cigars are generally made in Miami with Nicaraguan tobaccos but the Brown Label Tatuaje cigars for Europe and Asia, as well as some special editions, are made in Nicaragua. The Tatuaje Reserva Sir Winston (SW) from 2010 is a staggering masterpiece. It is rich and tasty but it sets itself apart with finesse. This cigar embodies that rare combination of strength and grace – imagine a football player perfectly executing a waltz.

Tatuaje, Havana VI

One of the iconic cigars which hoisted Pete and Pepin to the mantle of cigar makers who create art from rich Nicaraguan tobaccos, was the Tatuaje Havana VI. The Havana Six or Red Label cigars are made entirely in Esteli, Nicaragua of Nicaraguan tobaccos. Rich, powerful, interesting, complex, satisfying, these cigars seem to have it all.

For a powerful and highly flavourful companion for an afternoon espresso, choose one of the shorter *vitolas* such as the 4⅝" long Angeles. If you prefer a more refined and experiential smoke, choose something longer and with some heft, such as the Almirantes, a Churchill-sized piece of heaven.

» La Verite (The Truth)

Pete Johnson pokes the traditional cigar industry by constantly developing intriguing cigars and marketing concepts. His biggest gamble to date has been a project called La Verite.

The project is inspired by the similarities between the creation of cigars and fine wines. Whereas fine wines are made from a single plot of land and a single growing season, cigars are not. Cigars are blended with selections of tobacco from different areas and years. This allows producers a tremendous number of options when blending.

Pete's idea was to emulate vintage wine makers who have to create the taste of their wines in the field and in just a few barrels. In the case of La Verite, the cigars are crafted from tobaccos exclusively grown in the La Estrella (The Star) field of Nicaragua in 2008. Released two years after harvesting, these cigars are truly one of a kind.

The Churchill-sized La Verite is smooth and elegant. It inevitably captures the essence of the field. Both as a collector's item and as a fine cigar, La Verite deserves a place in your humidor.

Ashton

www.ashtoncigar.com

Ashton cigars are among the most prestigious in the world. When the super-premium cigar company tasted samples of Pepin's early cigars, they decided to meet the man himself in Miami. After a few meetings and many cigars, a deal was struck and Pepin began to make the creamy San Cristobal cigar for Ashton.

»

San Cristobal

The first effort these companies made together was a cigar that was markedly different from the cigars Pepin had been making previously. San Cristobal is Maduro wrapped and rather than being dominated by spice, this cigar is creamy. It has dense smoke, complex flavours and light sweetness. The best example of the brand's character is the Monumento.

»

Mi Amor

Le Snob ESSENTIAL La Aroma de Cuba's Mi Amor line was launched in 2010 and yet again, the pairing of Ashton and Pepin made waves. Mi Amor highlights tastes in tobacco that are rarely found. Its Mexican wrapper brings sweetness to a blend with a complex mixture of tastes from earthy to citrus. Flavour-bomb, taste explosion, however you want to characterise the cigar, this is one unique taste. What makes the cigar most remarkable is that the diverse flavours are brought together in a deliciously harmonious blend.

>> **La Aroma de Cuba**

La Aroma de Cuba, or as it is known outside the USA La Aroma del Caribe, has been Ashton's full-bodied, Central American cigar since 2002. Its strong flavour and modest price have made it very popular over the years. In 2008, Ashton asked Pepin to make a new La Aroma de Cuba (LADC) for them that they would call the Edicion Especial.

The LADC Edicion Especial is a milder smoke than the original LADC. It features well-balanced bready, nutty and spicy flavours. Its delivery is refined but it maintains that richness that comes from Nicaraguan tobacco.

Padron

Tel: +1(800) 453 5635, www.padron.com

For decades now, one brand of cigar has stood at the top of the Nicaraguan cigar industry. The company was there before the Sandinistas took over Esteli and they returned when it was safe. Because of the tobacco, Padron Cigars has stuck with Nicaragua and elevated its reputation with a time tested approach to quality.

Padron Cigars are wonderful. But the name Padron refers to the family as much or more than to the cigars. Jose Orlando Padron left Cuba in the early 1960s. He was born into the tobacco business and stayed in it even after leaving his homeland. Whereas in Cuba his family was in the leaf brokering game, in the USA and Nicaragua Jose Orlando got into the manufacturing game.

He started by making cigars for the local community in Florida. The cigars became more popular and as the company expanded, he was able to employ more of his family in the business. Today, the business looks like an elaborate family tree. 'But make no mistake,' Jose Orlando urges, 'each person has had to earn their position.'

'Orlando' as he is sometimes called, and his son Jorge (president of the company) are both very warm people. They instantly make friendships and happily share cigars. It is the cigars themselves that have earned Padron Cigars the most prestigious position in the world of Nicaraguan cigars.

Thousands Maduro and Natural

The classic line of Padron cigars is called the 'thousands' line because each size is named with a number such as: 1000, 2000, etc. Strictly this is not true, it is called the Padron series. But retailers and customers find that too confusing so they devised this alternate naming convention. Also in the 'thousands' series are cigars with plain *vitola* names such as Churchill, Panetela, Palmas and other traditional names.

Padron Series cigars are available with two wrappers, natural or Maduro. The natural cigars exhibit the tremendous earthiness that Nicaraguan tobacco can produce. Maduros, in this case, put a

Words from the wise

Michael Herklotz General Manager, Davidoff, USA

» Collectable cigars

Cigars generally aren't good as an investment, as although some cigars become more valuable with time, it only rarely happens. For those who want to have special and unique cigars just for the pleasure of owning them, or for special occasions, it is worth finding collectable cigars.

Regular production cigars can be collectable, as any cigar is a snapshot in the history of a brand, and while, theoretically, a brand of cigars is blended to taste the same every year, sometimes there is a change and that is what makes it interesting.

The more obvious place to start is with limited edition cigars. Truly limited cigars have a fixed quantity and when they are gone, they're gone, so if there's one you like, hoard it while you can. I also suggest buying cigars when they first come out, as that's when the manufacturer's intentions are clearest, when the preferred tobaccos are available.

fine, rich sweetness on the blend. The cigars remain highly flavourful and strong but gain finesse.

» Anniversary 1926 Maduro and Natural

When Jorge or Orlando want to create something truly exclusive, they designate it with the Anniversary 1926 band. 1926 commemorates the year Jose Orlando was born. The tobaccos in these cigars are aged at least one year longer than the 1964 line. But the real secret behind the magic of the 1926 cigars is selection. Jose Orlando selects the choicest and most interesting tobaccos for these cigars.

Nicaraguan dirt, in all its richness, flows up through the plant into the leaves and is present in

Cigar Zone in Esteli and Managua

As money splashes into Nicaragua, the country is changing. Esteli, the heart of cigar country, now has its own Miami-style nightclub – the ultra-modern and slick venue, Cigar Zone. This night club is a rarity, and is a great place to network, as well as to sip *flor de cano* rum or a cold Tona beer.

Another Cigar Zone thrives in the Las Americas Shopping Mall in Nicaragua's capital, Managua. Urbane and Miami-esque, the Managua Cigar Zone is popular and crowded. It features Nicaraguan cigars which are slurped up by the elite citizens of the capital. Both places represent the growing sophistication of Nicaraguan cigar smokers.

the 1926 blends. Known for richness, the 1926 are both refined and highly flavourful. Padron grows all their natural wrappers directly under sun, not hidden away. This brings more flavour to the leaves but it also makes them more coarse than other cigars. The rough appearance is all part of the charm as experienced smokers know that the thick leaf is packed with flavour.

» ### Anniversary 1964 Maduro and Natural

Le Snob ESSENTIAL Orlando has an 'old-school' approach to value which is obvious when the range of his cigars is viewed together. The cigars with the youngest tobacco and the least processing are the least expensive. Every cigar in the Anniversary 1964 range is filled with tobacco aged at least four years. This method requires a great investment and much planning for the future.

The result is spectacular. Whether you prefer the savoury main course of a natural wrapped, sun-grown Anniversary 1964, or the Moroccan version with hints of dates and sweet red fruit added to the plate (Maduro) you recognise the quality in these cigars.

Family Blend

Special project cigars have been coming out of Padron's Esteli factory every year for the past five years. At first it seemed that they were just flexing their creative muscles, but now a plan has emerged.

A cigar called the Family Blend has been released for the past few years. Each year the blend changes and the cigar is named after the company's anniversary. For example the 2010 cigar was the 46th anniversary. This is all leading up to the big moment when the company turns 50. Padron has been looking forward to this and have already begun fermenting the tobacco for the special cigar.

Family Blend cigars have all been delicious and collectors around the world have been saving them. In 2015 when the fiftieth-anniversary cigar is released, this will be a truly special occasion. Because of Padron's reputation, it is tempting to recommend buying without tasting. While that is never a good idea, the enjoyability of these Family Blend cigars is almost guaranteed.

Joya de Nicaragua

Tel: +505 2713 2758,
www.joyadenicaragua.com.ni

Joya de Nicaragua is the longest continuously producing cigar factory in Nicaragua. They are the only cigar makers who continued to produce during the Sandinista Revolution and who continued further during the American trade embargo. It was through enterprising local ownership that the brand survived.

Joya is a small brand with wide distribution. The flavour profile is unique and showcases the strength of the most powerful Nicaraguan tobaccos.

» Antano 1970

The Antano 1970 is the company's signature cigar and most well-known blend. Tastes that are bitter and sour can alienate some smokers, depending on flavour preferences, but this is one of the best non-Cuban cigars to age for a long term.

UNIQUE » RARE » LITTLE-KNOWN » ULTIMATE **Snob**

Vintage non-Cuban cigars Truly old cigars from Central America, Dominican Republic or Jamaica are virtually non-existent today.

In the 1970s, Joya de Nicaragua produced cigars which were stronger than anything else at the time. Because of their strong taste and durable tobaccos, those cigars from that period still smoke very well today. Much newer cigars such as Avelino Lara's Graycliff cigars from the early 1990s also smoke very well today. Padron and Fuente cigars from the 1980s are similarly excellent.

Most collector attention is focused on Habanos, so non-Cuban aged cigars are virtually unknown. This leaves the prices of aged non-Cuban cigars quite modest, usually only a small percentage higher than the prices of fresh cigars.

Oliva Cigars

www.olivacigar.com

Just ten years ago, Oliva Cigars was a small concern. It was a family business in which Gilberto was passing the company along to his four children. Then, as if overnight, the company began to change. Now it is one of the fastest-growing cigar companies in the world.

Its portfolio is remarkably complete with cigars ranging from mild to strong and skinny to fat. Yes, it is Oliva we have to thank for the craze over short, fat cigars. Sam Leccia, an Oliva salesperson in the United States wanted to experiment with cigar making. When he had created something unique and to his tastes, it was dubbed the NUB.

» NUB Cigars

The NUB is a new format for cigars. The concept is that cigars can burn slowly if they are very wide and densely filled with tobacco. A 4-inch cigar with a 60 ring gauge can burn as long as a cigar 50 per cent longer with a 48 ring gauge. This revelation propelled Oliva on to the front lines of cigar theory where it remains today.

» Cain Cigars

Sam Leccia's second contribution to the cigar world is a brand called Cain. This brand is based on another concept. Cain cigars feature tobaccos almost entirely composed of Ligero leaf. Ligero is extremely strong in flavour and nicotine and it burns very slowly. Knowing that, Sam built several blends and has sold Cain very well. The cigar market in the

Words from the wise

Abel Exposito Director, La Casa del Habano at the Partagas Factory, Havana

» Cigar festivals

I would recommend that all serious cigar lovers should go to a cigar festival at least once in their lives. As well as offering great entertainment, a festival is a unique opportunity to learn more about cigars and appreciate them in the company of other enthusiasts.

In Havana, smoking cigars is a very social activity. Once a year we invite our clients to come together in Havana to enjoy Partagas cigars and they come from all around the world.

At our annual festival, the mood is like the social and convivial VIP smoking lounge at the back of our store, where our best customers and aficionados smoke cigars together. The energy is high and the friendships formed around a cigar last a lifetime. The festival lasts for a week, giving people the chance to enjoy the best hotels and restaurants in Havana, as well as a day spent at the tobacco farms to delve deeper into the world of cigars.

USA is highly inquisitive and Leccia's innovations are feeding people's curiosity.

» Oliva Series V

Le Snob ESSENTIAL The series V is one of Oliva's many series denoted with a letter. V is the latest addition and it has come into the market at just the right moment. It is a full-flavoured, high-power cigar made entirely of Nicaraguan tobaccos. The wrapper is grown from Habano seeds under the full rays of the sun which bring out its flavour.

Its blend is more traditional than the NUB and Cain and it is oriented to a smoker who wants a classic cigar profile, executed to perfection. Since its release, this cigar has attained critical acclaim. While the Belicoso has taken a great deal of attention, the most elegant presentation of the blend is the Churchill *vitola*.

Plasencia

Tel: +1(305) 267 9717, www.sagimports.com

No chapter about Nicaraguan cigars can be completed without discussing the Plasencia family; in particular Nestor Senior and Junior. This father and son team are among the largest premium tobacco leaf growers in the world. In addition to leaf growing and pre-industrial processing, the Plasencias make cigars.

Most cigar enthusiasts have never heard of the Plasencias. They have heard of Rocky Patel, Maya Selva and Los Blancos cigars, all of which are made in Plasencia's factories. Currently there are two cigar brands that Plasencia is involved in marketing in addition to creating. One is Casa Magna and the other is Plasencia Reserva Organica.

» Casa Magna

Manuel Quesada teamed up with Nestor Plasencia to create a Central American-style cigar for his company based in the Dominican Republic. The result of these two men of tobacco teaming up was electric. The cigar, in both natural and Maduro, represents a refined version of well-fermented Central American tobacco.

» Plasencia Reserva Organica

Nestor Junior set a goal for himself. He wanted to create the first all organic cigar and he did! The Organica is grown in soil naturally fertilised and aerated by earthworms. It is cured in an exclusive barn then fermented in pilones apart from other tobacco. Finally it is blended and the result is a very good cigar. The taste is very clean with a light to medium body. Its aroma is woody and nutty and the taste is savoury and bready.

» **Rocky Patel 15th Anniversary**

In 2010, Rocky Patel built and opened a new factory in downtown Esteli. This break from his past, hiring others to roll for him, was timed with his fifteenth year in the cigar business. To commemorate the anniversary, Rocky created a cigar in his new facility called the 15th Anniversary. It is a triumph of Nicaraguan soil. Its complex taste of earth, nuts, chocolate and spice dances on the palate.

094

» Dominican Republic

Variety of style

Classy or hot, whichever style you prefer, it is rolled in the Dominican Republic. At the same high level as found in Cuba, many of the most prestigious cigar brands hail from the sun-blanketed island of the Dominican Republic.

Variety in styles

On one hand you have the old-world urbane style of Zino Davidoff and on the other, you have the Cuban gentlemanly style of the Fuente family. High-class events around the world prominently feature cigars from those two manufacturers.

The younger brother to the classically smooth Dominican style, is the Dominican Spice with its rebellious spirit. The tobacco, especially of the Habano 2000 and Piloto Cubano variety grown in direct sun on the island, exhibits tremendous amounts of flavour, much of it hot and spicy. The new millenium saw a rise in popularity of these types of cigar.

World-class producers

The Dominican Republic makes the largest number of premium cigars of any country in the world. Its total is now greater than Cuba and its produce is exported to nearly every country in the world.

The biggest producers on the island are those that produce for Altadis and General Cigar but also among the largest are A. Fuente y Cia., Davidoff (Tabadom), and many others that are large but not quite as large as these above who produce tens of millions of cigars per year.

Fuente y Cia

www.cigarfamily.com

The Arturo Fuente company knows what smokers want. They produce a portfolio that ranges from the smooth and easy Chateau series to the hot and heavy Opus X. In the middle are amazing varieties of Cameroon-wrapped beauties.

The company has been in existence since 1912 when Arturo Fuente began making cigars in Tampa, Florida out of Cuban tobacco. Through the generations the company has suffered many difficulties due to revolutions, loss of tobacco supplies and even fires. But through the one hundred years, the family stuck together and persevered. Cigar enthusiasts are the beneficiaries, as is evidenced by the variety of top-flight cigars Carlos and Carlito make today.

» **Opus X**

Most famous among the Fuente brands is the Opus X. It was released in 1995 and made waves for many reasons. The Fuente family is proud to say that it was the first Dominican cigar to be made entirely of Dominican tobacco. Indeed this was an accomplishment. What is more likely the cause of the cigar's success is its excellent blending and 'new school' taste.

It is a spicy firecracker of a cigar with huge power and a lot of nicotine. It was marketed superbly with a beautiful band designed by Vrijdag in the

Netherlands. The cigar came of age just as the number of people smoking cigars in the world was increasing. The 'cigar boom' of the late nineties featured the Opus X very prominently on the lips of tastemakers.

» Fuente Anejo

Le Snob ESSENTIAL A cigar that is also limited but is only known to the most discerning connoisseurs is called the Fuente Anejo. This cigar, as its name suggests, consists of tobaccos which have been well aged before they were rolled into the cigar. Because Carlos and Carlito determined to have an aged cigar with not only smoothness but also flavour, they created an instant classic. In any of its *vitolas* this cigar delivers bold, complex sweetness and very earthy tastes as a base.

La Aurora

Tel: +829 949 1903, www.laaurora.com.do

The oldest manufacturer in the Dominican Republic is La Aurora, owned by the Leon family. Since 1903, the traditional company has produced Dominican cigars with an unique identity. They are not trying to be Cuban.

It is hard not to think of La Aurora as a standard in the world of Dominican cigars. Maybe this is because they have been doing it longer than their neighbours or perhaps it is because they have developed a uniquely Dominican style that is very popular around the world.

» La Aurora 100 Anos

The Cien Anos, Spanish for, 100 years is one of the most spectacular cigars that La Aurora ever produced. Its Dominican wrapper covers a mostly Corojo set of fillers. It is a rich cigar with amazing complexity and savoury flavours.

This is the type of cigar that begs to be smoked without a strong drink. The cigar's flavours can be drunk on their own. Disappointingly, the cigar is limited in its production and may not be around much longer. One thing we can count on is La Aurora creating more cigars until they have found something to match it or possibly even surpass it.

» Making (and faking) a Maduro

The traditional method for processing a Maduro leaf
is to ferment a wrapper leaf at high temperatures for a
long period. The extended exposure to heat and
pressure darkens the leaf and brings out its sweetness.
If leaves are fermented too extremely they may begin
to deteriorate. The extra time spent in pilones and
not in cigars is also costly to the cigar maker, so some
producers employ shortcuts.

Some fake a dark colour by brushing tea, coffee or
dyes on to the leaves. Not only does this deny the
smoker the enjoyment of a well-fermented leaf, the
colour can also bleed out on to their lips.

Less controversial is a technique whereby leaves
are heated with ovens in order to mature them more
rapidly. The shortened fermentation time has a
downside: it does not allow the chemical process to
occur as completely, so the leaves do not reach their
peak smooth sweetness.

MATASA

Tel: +1(305) 267 9717, www.sagimports.com

The Dominican Fonseca brand is well known for its clean Connecticut wrappers and big taste underneath. The smooth Fonsecas are made by Manuel Quesada at his MATASA factory in Santiago, Dominican Republic. But a change is underfoot. A new generation of cigar makers, marketers and related professionals is finding their way in the business. They are all the children and cousins of Manuel and his partners. Their youth is causing the kind of activity that only unrelenting energy can bring. From this activity is springing new cigars.

» **Quesada Tributo**

Tributo, or Tribute, is a passionate cigar release from the Quesada's younger generation. It is a cigar line dedicated to the family members lost in a plane crash. Each *vitola* takes one of their passed family member's names: Manolin, Alvaro, Alvarito and Julio.

The cigar is a departure from the Connecticut-wrapped Fonsecas also made in the factory. These cigars are rich and strong. They are deliberately not smooth and they show the mindset of this younger generation. They are taking risks, making big bold flavours and showing their pride for the past.

Litto Gomez

Tel: +1(800) 543 7131, www.laflordominicana.com

One of the last decade's fastest-rising stars is Litto Gomez. He produces the La Flor Dominicana and Litto Gomez cigar lines from his factory in the Dominican Republic. He has taken a fast and high trajectory to his high position in the industry. His cigars are very popular and he is the leader of the 'strong cigars' movement. An afternoon with him in his factory will reveal his preferences.

The rollers' tables seem to be full of Ligero rather than a blend of leaves for production. The truth of the matter is that his cigars simply have mostly strong tobacco and lots of Ligero leaf accomplishes his goals. His style is like that of the Opus X in that he uses Dominican tobacco to produce strong spicy blends. As a maker with this specific preference he has created a wide variety of very strong blends.

>> ### La Flor Dominicana Salomon

Le Snob ESSENTIAL Almost certainly his best cigar, Litto's La Flor Dominicana Salomon, is an exquisite smoke. In this massive format, the cigar maker's preference for strength finds its ideal space.

The length and width allow the smoke to be cool and refined despite the strength of the tobacco. The blend he created perfectly balances the strength and flavour of the tobacco.

Spicy, earthy, a little sweet, somewhat herbal, but mostly it is just a great blend of tastes somewhat undefinable. This is the cigar most suitable to

UNIQUE » RARE » LITTLE-KNOWN » ULTIMATE **Snob**

Winston Churchill's cigars
Romeo y Julieta named a cigar 'Churchill' in honour of the man, but of all the cigars Winston smoked, records suggest that he rarely smoked from the Romeo y Julieta brand. He smoked cigars every day of his adult life, and would generally smoke less expensive Cuban cigars such as La Corona or Por Larranaga.

His personal cigars have surfaced at auctions and have fetched record prices above three and four thousand British Pounds. The chances of finding a cigar he owned available for purchase is extremely rare.

There are two places in the world that regularly display cigars formerly owned by the Prime Minister. A half-smoked cigar sits in the Cabinet War Rooms Museum in Westminster, and an entire box of his cigars, as well as his cutter, reside in the museum at the James J. Fox and Robert Lewis tobacconist in London.

listening to a long speech. It will allow you to go back and forth between paying attention to it and paying attention to the speaker, as you wish.

Davidoff and Tabadom

www.davidoff.com

Davidoff is the brand which spearheads the production of Tabadom in the Dominican Republic. As strong as the Davidoff name is, it is the man behind Tabadom who is best known in the Dominican Republic for Tabadom's cigars. His name is, of course, Henke Kelner. He is the Master Blender behind all the cigars that Tabadom makes.

The list is long: Davidoff, Zino, Avo, Griffins, Cusano and the dozens of sub-brands under each of these famous names. Henke is famous for his rigorous study of tobacco, the scientific processes behind tobacco fermentation and growing and mostly tasting. He holds tasting seminars which are extremely challenging to the participants.

The seminars are controversial for his claims about the process of perceiving taste. But at the end of one of his seminars, every participant will have been challenged to improve his 'palate' and ability to taste.

The character of the cigars blended by Henke is markedly different from those found at many other factories. His blends are extraordinarily well balanced and complex, though the novice may find them bland. The blending is done in such a way that there are no particularly strong flavours and yet the cigars are mysteriously satisfying and delicious.

Davidoff #1

When Zino Davidoff removed his production from Cuba, the Dominican Republic welcomed him with open arms. But he faced a difficulty. The tobacco available in the Dominican Republic was very different from the tobacco available in Cuba, due to the restrictions of the US trade embargo and Cuban protectionism/ state monopoly of tobacco. So he had to blend an entirely new set of cigars.

One of the most iconic Cuban Davidoff cigars was the #1. It is named for the Laguito #1 factory *vitola*. Today, the same size is produced in the Dominican Republic with finesse. The No. 1 lives in a world of elegance. It is long, slender, constructed perfectly and finished with a classic, clean white and gold band. The band is a reminder of the brand's Cuban past. The band was initially chosen from one of the stock bands that Cuba would use when making a cigar especially for an individual. They would take the stock band and place the person's name or image in the middle. Davidoff's band evolved from that initial art by subtly embossing the gold and artfully designing the script.

As for the taste, which is what most smokers care about, the #1 is lovely. It has a creamy character and a fresh acidity that keeps the palate clean. Throughout the long smoke, spices and light earthy flavours reveal themselves. Few cigars can compete with the Davidoff #1 for elegance.

General Cigar

Swedish Match Company, USA

Tel: +1(804) 302 1700, www.cigarworld.com

Benji Menendez is the Master Blender for General Cigar in the Dominican Republic. Hailing from the family that once owned Montecristo and H. Upmann in Cuba, Benji now blends the Partagas, Cohiba and Macanudo cigars for General Cigar, among others.

General Cigar's Dominican stable of cigars is becoming more and more formidable every year. Under Benji's stewardship, the company is releasing cigars with a more modern style than many competitors. The Partagas brand has been a particular focus for Benji as he has introduced the Partagas Spanish Rosado, Partagas Black Label and many special editions.

» **Partagas Master Series by Benji Menendez**

Le Snob ESSENTIAL The Dominican Partagas with the Benji Menendez signature on the bottom is one not to be missed. As Benji says, it is a cigar that he prefers to smoke. It has much of the character of the spicy Dominican Partagas blend but with a twist. In this case, the twist comes in the form of leaves designed to deliver sweetness and earth to the blend. For the smoker, this means that the cigar is rich, full flavoured, medium strength and marvellously complex.

» **Macanudo 1968**

Another brand to receive a great deal of Benji's attention has been Macanudo. This formerly Jamaican brand has been one of the world's most popular cigars for years. Its character suits the majority of smokers, being mild and tasty. But that is the original lines of Macanudo.

In 2008, the Macanudo 1968 was launched and while many people expected another mild cigar with refined flavour, they were shocked when they smoked it. The 1968 is really not in the character of Macanudo. It has a big flavour, excellent fermentation and more obvious flavours than any preceding Macanudo. The big tastes are sweet, earthy and altogether much more in line with the new school of cigar blending. Benji is a leader among the group of cigar makers catering to the new style of big, bold cigar blends.

Altadis

Tabacalera de Garcia, USA

Tel: +1(888) 262 2511, www.altadisusa.com

In the most beautiful beach community in the Dominican Republic sits the cigar factory that produces millions of 'Cuban Legacy' brands such as Romeo y Julieta, Montecristo and H. Upmann, brands which originated in Cuba and are now produced elsewhere. The company is called Tabacalera de Garcia and it is operated by the Master of Tobacco, Jose Siejas.

Words from the wise

Valerio Cornale Propietor of La
Casa del Habano, Cayman Islands

» Back to basics

My advice for cigar smokers who would like to start
to try rarer and more exclusive cigars is to start with
the basics. For example, most of the best Habanos
made today are regular lines. The H. Upmann Sir
Winston, Cohiba Esplendido and Montecristo No. 2
are all classics, but most smokers forget about them.

The problem is that many people want to go after
the newest cigars, and while some of those are great,
not all are as good as the regularly produced ones.
Cigars such as the Cohiba Sublime from 2004 and
the Cohiba Behike are simply fantastic.

It is not that there are no good limited editions
being released, but there are so many great cigars
available every day that there is little reason to chase
the limited ones. So when someone asks me about
smoking a rare cigar, I point them to a classic that
they have not smoked in a while.

Siejas is a life-long tobacco man who is soft spoken and a genius when it comes to blending mild cigars. His recent Santa Damiana Puro Dominicana is an extraordinary example of how tasty a mild cigar can be when blended by an expert, with extremely high-quality tobaccos.

» Santa Damiana

Perhaps the most interesting cigar made by Siejas in La Romana, Dominican Republic is the brand Santa Damiana. It is not the largest brand, in fact it is not very well known. But it delivers a very well-designed bowl of flavours in a medium-strength package. The blend is elegant and highly enjoyable. The cigar received the ECJ Cigar Trophy in 2009 for Best Value, Dominican Republic.

» Possess

Collecting cigars

Cigar enthusiasts want to learn about and see interesting cigars. In a sense, that is the defining characteristic of a cigar enthusiast. The difficulty of this task lies in the cost of the most interesting cigars. Some of the rarest can cost thousands of dollars per stick, and clearly that is not something that most cigar smokers will want to pay.

An item of beauty

Despite the cost of these cigars, it is the goal of many cigar enthusiasts to obtain some collectable cigars. There is nothing quite like the visual appeal of a rare-aged cigar on the top row of a desktop humidor. Its finish has dulled from age, and it stands out from the rest of the smokeable beauties as something special, something that has been cherished and saved.

Is it possible for the average connoisseur with a modest budget to obtain cigars worth cherishing? The answer is yes. With a little creativity and knowledge, enthusiasts such as myself have gone from smoker to smoker/collector. Once you know the important categories that collectable cigars fall into, and how to spot the ones worth having, it becomes easier to expand your collection. For more information see pages 44 (dating a cigar), 85 (identifying collectable cigars) and 89 for vintage cigars).

Collector's categories

The first thing to note is that there are essentially three categories of cigars as the collector sees it. There are Aged, Rare, and Production cigars. Each is collected for different reasons and the value is assigned for different reasons. To understand this is to be able to estimate a cigar's value.

Aged cigars

Aged cigars are those cigars which were rolled at least five years before now. No serious collector says that they have aged cigars which have been 'resting' for six months. It is ridiculous. What makes a cigar aged is the microfermentation that the cigar experiences once it has been rolled.

Tobacco is heavily fermented in order to remove the vast amount of its impurities, including nicotine. This occurs before the leaf is rolled into a cigar. Once the various leaves have been combined in the finished cigar, there are small amounts of fermentable material left in the tobacco. Therefore the cigar can still ferment.

When a cigar ferments in its box, it is a gentle process. It changes very little and it takes years for a noticeable change to occur. But when the change happens it is unmistakeable. Aged cigars mellow over time and as some stronger tastes subside, more subtle tastes emerge. This is the magic of aging, and it doesn't happen in six months.

Rare cigars

Rare cigars are simply understood. It is hard to find them because not many exist. Often times, a manufacturer will create only a small supply of a certain cigar in order to ensure its rarity. Usually called 'Limited Editions', these cigars are easily identifiable as rare.

But other rarities exist and are often more interesting for example the Culebra (see box below), which are limited in the number produced because it takes a very specialised roller to create them. The cigar maker who created a cigar that put him out of business may have just created a rare cigar. In this

Sharing a Culebra

There is nothing quite like the experience of smoking a Culebra with friends. Culebras are three cigars, twisted together while still moist. The result is a peculiarly curvy presentation.

The origin of this peculiar cigar shape is contested. Common to most stories of the history of the culebra is that it was a cigar for the *torcedors*. Some say the cigars were curved to prevent rollers from smoking cigars meant for sale. Another story claims that the curved cigars were meant to keep track of how many cigars a roller would smoke. Whatever the reason for its creation, today it is a most unique shape and one ideally suited for the unashamed and highly sociable enthusiast.

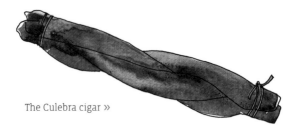
The Culebra cigar »

case the cigar production was limited and there is an interesting story to go along with its exclusivity.

These days there are dozens of manufacturers creating limited quantities of cigars at high prices. This small-batch production is interesting and good for sales, but the glut of them on the market has made it difficult to know which ones are worth buying and which ones are not. Ironically, the supply of limited cigars has increased. So rather than increasing values due to scarcity, the values remain the same as regular production cigars in many cases.

Regular production

The cigars we see every day and have been produced for years are called Regular Production. These are our Montecristo No. 2s and Ashton Classics. Taste wise, these are often the best and most consistent cigars in a given year. But the predictability of their price and availability causes them to not be collector's cigars unless they have been aged for a significant period.

Buying cigars

Buying collectible cigars is more difficult than it may at first appear. There are laws that complicate any cross-border sale. Tobacco taxes can be very confusing and they vary from country to country and state to state. You'll need to investigate the costs and regulations before you look into buying anything. Complicating matters more is the American embargo of Cuban products which restricts the trade of Cuban cigars made after 1961 when an American is on one side of the transaction. But these are the obvious challenges.

Assessing the product

The less obvious issue at stake is the assessment of authenticity and quality, to make sure you know what you are buying, and are paying a reasonable price for it. Cigars stored in dry conditions or sunlight are likely to have no taste left within. If a collector wants to buy a collectible cigar for smoking, not just setting on a shelf, he should find a way to assess its smokeability.

Then of course there are those unscrupulous sellers who would fool buyers by mislabelling cigars. In recent years the instance of counterfeit cigars and re-banded cigars has increased on the collector's market. It sounds daunting but despite the hazards, there are ways to build your collection in a relatively safe way.

Words from the wise

Mitch Orchant Antique
buyer, C.Gars Ltd, UK

›› Vintage cigars

In most pre-Castro Cuban cigars, the complexity is
gone, and it becomes an entirely new smoking
experience as compared with current production. A
recent cigar may be improving or at its peak, whereas
an old cigar is either maintaining or going downhill.
Some cigars from particular brands will age better
than others. Those with darker wrappers, heavier
blends and more oily wrappers will always age longer
and better than those with a lighter wrapper and a
lighter blend.

Pre-Castro cigars are for a very particular person. If
you are not an experienced smoker of Cuban cigars,
I wouldn't recommend a vintage Havana cigar. If
one were to try such a cigar for the first time, I
suggest smoking it on a clean palate, with a
complementary drink, ideally something palate
cleansing. They should smoke it alone, in quiet, so
that they can appreciate the unique flavour.

Aged and rare cigars

The Aged and Rare segments of the market are the most treacherous. This is where you will find cigars that were aged in a shoebox being sold at top prices. You may also find a perfectly round 'Davidoff from Cuba' with a bright oily and aromatic wrapper leaf – or so you are told. In reality, a genuine 20-year-old cigar will no longer be perfectly round and brightly oily, life in its box will have aged its appearance. It's important to be very careful and very sure of the product before you buy.

Question the seller

Determining if a cigar is in good smokeable condition is not easy. Two investigations should be made. Firstly, ask the seller how the cigars have been stored. 'How long have you had the cigars? Did you buy them directly from a retailer ten years ago? In what did you store them? Were the cigars ever outside of your wine cellar for a long time?' Any shocks to the cigars, including sunlight and dry or hot air, will compromise the taste of the cigars. It will not usually zap them of all flavour but it will be diminished.

Examine the product

The second investigation should be physical. Pick up a cigar from the box. Does the paper band appear aged? Has the tobacco oil stained the paper? Did the foil corrode? Does the cigar look like it was compressed in the box since it was bought? Over time, cigars will change their shape. Most aged cigars have flattened sides from being squeezed into a box with twenty-five or fifty other cigars. Squeeze it between your fingers, does it make a loud crackling noise? You should be able to tell how dry the cigar is by doing this.

Any cigar that has a smokeable taste will give off an aroma. When the flavour is gone, the aroma is gone. So if you stick your nose into the cigar box and it is full of tobacco scents, you are in luck. That box of cigars is likely to still be tasteful.

Fake cigars

Some makers of counterfeit cigars are highly sophisticated. Their productions are likely to fool most smokers. Recently there has been a series of counterfeits made by placing actual aged cigar bands from valuable cigars on brand new cigars. The cigar dimensions were perfect and the band was authentic. The problem is that the cigar was not what it was purported to be.

Spotting a fake

Most fakes use reproduced bands placed on inexpensive cigars. Fortunately, most creators of fakes are lazy and they make mistakes. Whenever buying rare cigars that can be researched, it is advantageous to do so. Most cigar bands can be found online so to be sure that a band is authentic, a little research pays off. More than that, some simple measurements of ring gauge and length can reveal errors that are not easy for the eye to catch.

Where to buy

There are many reasons to be careful but it is impossible to build a collection without buying a few cigars.

Buy new

The safest way to ensure the quality and authenticity of your cigars is to purchase them from an authorised retailer. If you want aged cigars, then using this method you will need to age them yourself. This is not practical for the thirty-year-old who wants to smoke pre-embargo Havana cigars but it is the safest method to ensure you get what you're paying for.

Trusted vendors

Without buying every cigar new, there are still ways to reasonably guarantee that you will receive authentic and high-quality products. That is to find and use a trusted retailer. Most retailers of vintage and rare cigars are perfectly respectable and upstanding people. But there are a few sharks out there so it pays to build a relationship with a retailer.

Finding a good vendor of aged or rare cigars is tricky. Referrals from other collectors who have purchased from them in the past can be one of the best ways to find your vendor. Look around your area and discuss what you would like to collect with your local merchant. They are likely to come across things from time to time that might be of interest to you.

International retailers

While your local dealer is generally the best person with whom to build a relationship, there are some trustworthy retailers outside of your area who you can start with. There are retailers worldwide, below is a selection from a few key areas. In all cases, these retailers do not have the lowest prices. What they have is quality, supply and trustworthiness.

C.Gars Ltd. London
Suite 7048 Sheperd Market, Mayfair, London, W1J 7JY, UK, Tel: +44(0)700 008 8088, www.cgarsltd.co.uk

Davidoff London
35 St James's Street, London, SW1A 1HD, UK
Tel: +44(0)207 930 3079

Casa del Habano Teddington
76 High Street, Teddington, TW11 8JD, UK
Tel: +44(0)208 977 3793

Gerard Pere et Fils Switzerland
Grand Hôtel Kempinski, Quai du Mont Blanc 19
1201 Geneva, Switzerland, Tel: +41(0)22 908 35 35

Casa del Habano Berlin
Fasanenstraße 9, 10623 Berlin, Germany
Tel: +49(0)303 11 03 646, www.casa-del-habano.de

Casa de Puros Nurnburg
Hauptmarkt 9, 90403 Nürnberg, Germany
Tel: +49(0)911 97 46 690, www.casadelhabano.de

De La Concha, NYC
1390 Avenue of the Americas, New York, 10019, USA
Tel: +1(212) 757 3167

Sabor Havana, Miami
2600 NW 87th Ave, Doral, Florida 33172, USA
Tel: +1(305) 436 8860

Tobacco Grove, Maple Grove
8063 Wedgewood Ln N, Maple Grove, MN 55369, USA
Tel: +1(763) 494 6688, www.tobaccogrove.com

Buy in person

If the above options are not practical, perhaps the cigars of your desire are only available from one seller, then there is only one line of defence. Physically inspecting the cigars by looking, smelling, squeezing and asking questions of the seller is the only way to ascertain quality and authenticity. For the inexperienced buyer, this can be daunting. It is always useful to bring an experienced friend or to at least use the internet on a mobile device to research the bands once you are in front of the cigars.

Import restrictions and associated taxes

If you are purchasing your collectible cigars in another country or state, you will need to figure the cost of transferring them into your purchase price. The tax regulations that surround tobacco products seem to change every year. When purchasing cigars, it is always smart to read the current laws regarding purchase and transfer. On a government website, most countries have clearly defined the quantity of cigars you may ship or transport.

One of the increasingly aggravating traps laid by lawmakers is limits on the quantity of cigars allowed to cross borders. Before you travel anywhere, read the laws of your country and the countries you will visit to make sure that you will not be taxed or have your prized cigars confiscated. Mexico and much of Europe are particularly difficult places to enter with several boxes of cigars.

Breaking laws related to cigars can cause your favoured hobby to become the cause of your incarceration or at least a bother.

Correct storage

Cigars should be kept in a humidor, a box which contains a few dozen cigars and keeps a constant humidity and temperature, to maintain the quality of the product. Every enthusiast knows, from experience, that a cigar burns best when it is kept in a humid environment. The cigar should be moist enough that when squeezed, it does not crack, but not so wet that it does not burn.

Unfortunately, decades of cigar writers have perpetuated the myth that relative air humidity must be modified dramatically as temperatures change. According to the popular myth, if temperatures rise to 25°C (77°F), the relative humidity should be lowered to 56 per cent. Anyone who has ever followed this advice has ended up with a pile of dried flakes in the humidor.

Results of poor storage

The risks of poor storage are great. Not only are cigars at risk of poor burning in the short term, but there are long-term consequences as well. Cigars which have been dried out at some date but were rehumidified will not taste as strong as they otherwise would. The thinnest leaves will have had their oils dried. The loss of those oils will result in a cigar tasting only of the thickest leaves at the centre of the bunch.

Ideal conditions

Fortunately the solution is simple. Between the temperatures of 18 and 24°C (65 and 75°F), cigars can be kept at a standard relative humidity around 65 to 70 per cent. Since this covers most room temperatures, this is not difficult. To be certain that cigars are being kept correctly, simply open the humidor and look inside. As long as no moisture is visible, the top of the limit has not been surpassed. Squeeze the cigars – as long as they do not crack and return to their shape, they have not become too dry. Within this temperature and humidity range, cigars are being kept correctly and should last well.

To further avoid the difficulties of temperature and humidity spikes, they should be kept in an environment that excludes sunlight, warm lights and cold surfaces. By keeping cigars constantly in such conditions, their lives will be extended as long as the tobacco will permit, often more than 20 years.

Separate humidors

Some enthusiasts keep humidors at home segregated by country of manufacture, for example, one just for Cuban cigars – each country's tobacco has a unique signature, so when the enthusiast's mood requires a spicy sun-grown chilli pepper of a cigar, it is time to open the humidor filled with Dominican cigars.

In terms of correct storage, some people will keep a separate humidor specially designated for collectible cigars. Every collector has a few cigars that are only to be smoked on special occasions, and these rare cigars should be watched with eagle eyes. The slightest change in humidity necessitates corrective action because these are limited editions, aged or sentimental cigars.

Words from the wise

Fabien Garrigues Ex-cigar sommelier

» Matching cigars and drinks

Taste is very subjective and a perfect match is very difficult to accomplish. Most people match drinks with similar flavours and/or aromas to the cigar in order to develop the taste of the cigar. The idea is that tastes will not clash and will pair well when they are most similar.

I have been working behind bars for many years and I enjoy balancing flavours. I try to compliment the flavour expressed in the cigar by adding the missing flavour through the drink to create a perfect balance. For example, I love to match a full-flavoured Belgian beer with a powerful and dry cigar.

I recommend orangy/spicy rums with woody/nutty cigars. Havana Club Barrel Proof and a Montecristo Edmundo would be a good example. But there is no shortage of creative pairings. I have had very interesting pairings with beer, wine, spirits and non-alcoholic drinks – it comes down to personal taste.

Pairing cigars and drinks

At the Festival del Habano, the world's best cigar sommeliers put forth their ideas about the optimal combinations of Cuban cigars and drinks. Scotch, cognac, rum, even wine and exotic liquors are paired with cigars of strengths from light to strong. Each contestant at the Habano-Sommelier Competition has unique ideas about the best way to bring about delicious taste combinations. What they all avoid is a clash. Clashing tastes are easy to recognise. You won't see limoncello paired with a savoury cigar just like you won't see steak paired with strong lemon sauce at a fine restaurant. Theories abound as to the best pairing of cigars and drinks.

Understanding matching flavours

Most importantly you need to understand the principles behind a good pairing. Matching flavours, such as a bitter cigar with coffee is highly desirable – during the daytime, this is one of the most popular pairings. A nutty cigar will often be paired with a lightly roasted coffee with milk. In evenings, cigar passionados often get creative – they try the alternative method of complementing flavours. They will pair a sweet and spicy sprit like cognac or whisky with a complex savoury cigar to create an overall taste in the mouth that is unlike anything achieved by the cigar or spirit alone.

Cigar paraphernalia

Since collectible cigars must reside in tightly controlled climactic conditions to keep them at their best, collectors often decorate their spaces with cigar-related items that are also collectable. This allows a collector to be reminded of the treasures of the humidor while not ruining them with the sun's rays, heat or poor humidity.

Some of the most popular include cigar box art and cigar containers themselves. Entire books have been written on cigar art lithography. It can be beautiful and old examples capture a perspective of history that in other contexts is considered unfashionable.

Most of what is collected is old. Antique cigar jars, large cabinets used for shipping cigars and lithographs from cigar boxes are the most popular items used for home decor. But new items are

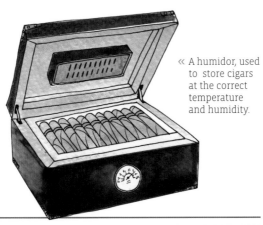

« A humidor, used to store cigars at the correct temperature and humidity.

becoming very popular. Artists, both professional and amateur, have developed a style of art that utilises cigar bands to create large works of art.

In some examples, they pattern the bands on a canvas and create an image composed of the smaller bands. Amateur artists have covered tabletops, lamps and lighters with the most brilliant cigar bands with exciting results.

State of collecting

At the moment, collectible cigars and accessories are in a renaissance. The base of collectors is growing. While not many of them are buying in the high end of the market, there is little doubt that some of them will make it there in the coming years and some very exciting auctions will result.

Because manufacturers are making so many rare and exclusive cigars, this is an excellent time for collectors. Intriguing cigars of today could be auction showpieces of tomorrow. But whether you sell them or smoke them, the acquisition and enjoyment of collectible cigars is a great way to extend one's knowledge in the hobby.

» Discover

Cigar travel

How do you make the leaves stick together in that shape with just water and a dab of vegetable gum? Why doesn't the thing just fall apart? Some questions are best answered by the practitioners, or better, on site. Gathering around the artisans and farmers who create cigars is a great learning experience.

Cigar production is magical. At each step, a seemingly miraculous transformation takes place. Unfortunately, the process is largely hidden from the connoisseur.

Visiting the factories

Only the Partagas, Romeo y Julieta and Pinar del Rio factories in Cuba have smoking lounges attached. Visitors to all other factories are met with locked gates and security guards. The best way to check out the world of cigar production is to travel on an organised trip.

Festivals and tours are the two primary ways that people get into cigar factories. Tours are the most educational. The most common type of tour is the kind offered by manufacturers. They will bring people down to their factory, for a fee, and show them how they create their cigars. It is a heady affair. Participants are bathed in premium cigars and good food. Some of the companies who offer tours to connoisseurs include Rocky Patel, Camacho, Los Blancos, Drew Estate and Davidoff.

Enthusiasts who want to see more than one factory can book a tour with Cigar Tourism. This company organises tours in Nicaragua and the Dominican Republic, and offers the chance to see multiple factories and tobacco fields, and hear different perspectives from company owners during a trip.

Traveller advice

It is easy to see tobacco growing. A car and a map are all a person needs. Simply drive to Pinar del Rio, Jalapa, or any other growing region and you will find yourself surrounded by the luscious leaf from January to March.

Tobacco farmers are a friendly lot and are usually approachable. Because of the attention to detail required by tobacco, you are likely to find a farm owner in the field. He will be happy to walk you through the plants. Perhaps the best way to see tobacco fields is simply to arrive, wear boots and politely ask to speak with the Jefe, or boss.

Useful contacts

For tours the following are useful starting points.

Cigar Tourism www.cigartourism.com
Tours multiple factories during each trip to cigar countries, Nicaragua, Dominican Republic, Honduras.

Camacho www.camachocigars.com
Tour Camacho farms and factory in Honduras.

Rocky Patel www.rockypatel.com
Tour where Rocky Patel cigars are made in Honduras as well as tobacco fields.

Los Blancos www.losblancos.com
Tour factory and fields that spawn Los Blancos cigars in Nicaragua.

Cigar festivals

Cigar smokers have gotten together in large groups for over a century. Banquets of yesteryear are the herfs of today. The sociability that cigars inspire causes large events to occur organically. But marketers could not leave cigar events to the enthusiasts.

The first country to organise an event for enthusiasts was Cuba. And for over a decade, Cuba was the only country to organise an event. Since 2008, the other three big cigar-producing countries have gotten organised and each has created their own festival, more or less successfully.

The longest-running cigar festivals happen annually in Cuba. One is for friends of Partagas and the other is for fans of all Habanos. Even if you don't perfectly fit into one of these categories, you will likely have a great time at the events during these week-long celebrations.

Encuentros de Clientes y Amigos de La Casa del Habano Partagas

Good customers and friends of the cigar store in the Partagas factory gather every year in November for a week of cigar smoking and socialising. Some 100–200 enthusiasts turn out each year for the festivities that range from beach days to factory tours and elaborate dinners.

The Partagas event is more intimate than its big brother, the Festival del Habano. It feels something like a class reunion. The week-long schedule begins with an opening dinner and entertainment. During the course of the week's events, commemorative cigars are handed out. The bands on these special cigars only dress the cigars given as part of the festival that week. This is a particular highlight. Participants have, over the years, gathered all the exclusive cigars with their unique bands and now have highly enviable collections.

During the week, the group spends one day at the beach in Varadero. This day is meant to be purely fun, and it is. Games are organised, fresh seafood is served and daiquiris, mojitos and Cuba libre's are all close at hand. Also mid-week is a day spent on the farms of Pinar del Rio. On this day the groups visit tobacco farms and talk with experts about the process of growing premium tobacco leaf.

Finally, the week wraps up with a gala dinner held in one of the event rooms in a top Havana hotel. This is the best attended event of the week, aside from smoking in the factory's VIP smoking lounge. The dinner features live entertainment, more cigars, a more formal atmosphere and recognition of all the VIP participants.

Festival del Habano

The biggest event of all is the annual Festival del Habano. Every February Havana plays host to over one thousand cigar enthusiasts from all around the world. This festival contains seminars, tastings and elegant events staged throughout the city of Havana.

The Festival del Habano is famous for having started as a small event held at the Tropicana Cabaret and annually at other exotic locations around Havana. In the early years, Fidel Castro would even show up to the gala dinner and sign a few cigar boxes for the charity auction. The thrill of outdoor events and Castro sightings still electrifies the festival even now that the gala dinner is held indoors and Fidel is unlikely to attend again. There are three parts to the festival; daytime events, evening events and the gala dinner.

Daytime events take place at the Palace of Conventions just outside Havana. Every day there are speakers, demonstrations, tastings and activities in the seminar rooms. It is here that the International Habanos Sommelier competition finals take place, historians of the Habano and the Cuban cigar industry give lectures, and expert tasters lead groups through tastings of vintage cigars, Armagnac, tequila and other selected spirits.

Also during the day, some 30 exhibitors display their goods in the Convention Palace. There you can find Cuban coffee and rum, but much more interestingly, humidors and other handcrafts. Antiques dealers display pre-embargo and aged cigar bands for sale. Top-level craftsmen bring their most intricate humidors for display.

The energy is ramped up in the evenings when Habanos puts on its shows. At the

« Commemorative case released for the festival.

beginning of the festival there is a welcome show which usually features some world-class performers, dramatic dance numbers and exciting music. After the opening show, where new products are announced, a drinks and cigar reception finishes off the night.

Another night during the week, a new cigar is usually launched. The attendees are the first members of the public to have a chance to smoke the cigar and it is always done in a beautiful setting. For several years, this event has been held on Wednesday evening at Club Havana – the exclusive beach club just outside Havana.

Finally, there is the gala dinner. This is the most extravagant event held in Cuba all year, lasting six hours. It begins with a welcome cocktail and cigar. Throughout the meal, diners can expect several more cigars between courses including a sample of the most exclusive new offering from Habanos for that year.

Capping the night is a charity auction. Proceeds go to benefit the Cuban health-care system. Simon Chase is the auctioneer, who has slowly increased overall bids to over one million dollars a year for massive and exclusive humidors full of cigars.

The Festival del Habano is the cigar event that every enthusiast should attend once in their lifetime. No other event has reached this status yet but one festival is getting close: Procigar.

Procigar

In 2008, the first in-country celebration took place outside of Cuba. Here comes the Dominican Republic! Under the auspices of Pro-cigar, a manufacturer organisation, a spectacular event was held in the style of the Festival del Habano.

Procigar, as it is called, lasts for one week and has a uniquely Dominican feel. Its member manufacturers, La Aurora, Altadis, General Cigar, Davidoff, Jean Clemente and MATASA each open their factories to attendees during the week. This is one of the two biggest differences between Procigar and the Festival del Habano, attendees can visit all the factories. Since each factory is owned by someone with a unique philosophy towards cigar making, touring from factory to factory is fascinating.

But Procigar is not just about factories, it is about Dominican culture. And the aspect of Dominican culture that stands out above its comparator in Cuba is the food. Dominican food is spectacular. Every day and every night the Procigar group organises spectacular meals. Slow-cooked meat, fresh fruit, spicy rum and dark coffee serve to make every meal at Procigar excellent.

By comparison, Procigar is just as well organised as the Festival del Habano and the food is better. Its focus is cigar makers. The Procigar festival is fast becoming a must-do event in a cigar enthusiast's life.

Festival del Tabaco

Nicaraguan cigar makers held their first festival in 2010. It had a strange mix of events. There were tours that seemed aimed at novices and there were seminars about investment in Nicaragua. But the meals, as one expects in Nicaragua, were excellent. The best fillet mignon were showcased alongside chimichurri or jalapeno sauce.

The festival does have a major hurdle to jump. There is only one hotel in Esteli that is considered satisfactory by most visitors. This means that there is an extreme shortage of beds and thus a limited number of people who can attend. But that may not be the biggest problem the festival has. At the moment it has neither a website nor any full-time staff.

Once they get the details and organisation figured out, this could be one of the best events to attend. But for now, most passionados of Nicaraguan cigars are waiting to see what will happen.

Humo Jaguar

There is not much to say about the Honduran cigar festival called 'Humo Jaguar'. At the time of this manuscript's completion, the first event in Honduras has not been completed. It is planned for spring 2011 and the organisers have explained that they want this event to be more elegant than many of the others. Organisers want to encourage visitors from outside the cigar world in order to have a diverse set of participants.

Festival contacts

Habanos Festival and Partagas Festival

www.habanos.com

Partagas

Tel: +537 862 3772 / +537 866 8060 / +537 860 8295

Email: partagas@tuhv.cha.cyt.cu

Procigar

http://procigar.org

Clubs and societies

Gatherings closer to home can be just as entertaining as festivals, if not quite as educational. If the local tobacconist is the lifeblood of the enthusiast community, the local cigar club is the heart. Local clubs keep the passion flowing and bring their members to a greater appreciation of this artisanal product.

Cigar clubs organise gatherings for members to enjoy cigars together. Sometimes they have a clubhouse and sometimes they meet at changing locations. As smoking bans increase, so do cigar clubs. Some clubs have even begun to work together to support each other.

In Italy, for example, the cigar clubs across the country have created a structure which allows all the clubs to communicate. It is called the Cigar Club Association (CCA). Through CCA, members know about other clubs' events and it promotes fraternity among all of the clubs in the country.

Cohiba Cigar Divan

Mandarin Oriental Hotel, Hong Kong

Tel: +852 2522 0111

At the Mandarin Oriental, the Cohiba Cigar Divan is an upscale lounge open to the public with a vast selection of rare aged cigars as well as the newest exclusive Habanos.

Club Pasion Habanos

Casa de America, Madrid, Tel: +34(915) 954 800

An intimate modern lounge in a grand stone building is one of the most special cigar spots in Madrid. Finding the lounge requires navigating the halls of the Casa de America but it is worth it for highly skilled bar tenders and a limited selection of the very best premium cigars.

Metropolitan Cigar Society, NY

Fairfield, New Jersey, Tel: +1(973) 287 6078

This is a vast, vibrant and highly-populated club just across Manhattan in New Jersey. It was started by enthusiasts and remains a haven for many cigar lovers.

Boisdale of Belgravia, London

15 Eccleston Street, London SW1W 9LX

Tel: +44(0)207 730 6922

Whisky, wine, aged steaks, live jazz and cigars are all found at the Boisdale of Belgravia in the heart of London. Atop the roof of the club a lounge was built that feels indoors despite being technically outdoors. The menu of cigars is vast though not as weighty as its whisky and wine menus, which number hundreds of pages. Always a boisterous crowd.

La Casa del Habano

Quinta Avenida, Havana, Cuba

Tel: +537 204 7973

Of the many places in Cuba to smoke a cigar, La Casa del Habano on 5th Avenue is one where serious enthusiasts always gather. Their selection is massive but more importantly they have a full bar and restaurant on site which enables cigar lovers to spend a full day there, which often happens.

Berliner Cigarren Club unter den Linden

Imperial Courts 1st Hof, 10117 Berlin

www.berliner-cigarren-club.de

Offering people the opportunity to gather and appreciate cigars in their smoking lounge, the club also aims to promote cigar culture, and organises tastings, seminars and other events around the city.

Online cigar clubs

Internet-based clubs or cigar forums allow members to communicate from far afield. They are great for smokers who live remotely or for enthusiasts who just want to discuss a specific type of cigar. In the end, the online cigar clubs wind up doing the same thing that the others do. They facilitate communication, meet-ups and stimulate passion for the hobby. So as cigar companies become more savvy, the opportunities to discover the origins of cigars grow.

Glossary

Aged cigar The proper term for a cigar which has been rolled many years ago. Sometimes incorrectly called vintage, aged cigars mellow in flavour with age. A cigar is typically only considered aged once it has existed for more than five years. Serious collectors of aged cigars often will not deem them aged with under ten years age.

Band Most cigars come dressed with a ring of paper one or two inches below the cigar's head. This paper is called a 'band' and it often reveals information about the cigar's maker or brand.

Binder The tobacco leaf that holds the filler in shape and sits under the wrapper is the Binder. It is often a leaf that is very elastic and less beautiful than wrapper leaf.

Blend The combination of leaves rolled together in a cigar make up its blend.

Cap The tobacco which sits at the head of a cigar. On *parejo* cigars the cap is a round piece of tobacco. On pyramids, the leaf finishes the point at the head of the cigar.

Chaveta The D-shaped blade a *torcedor* uses to cut tobacco while rolling a cigar.

Fermentation In tobacco, fermentation refers to the chemical process that makes tobacco smokeable. Sugars, water, heat and pressure cause a chemical reaction which removes nicotine and other compounds naturally found in tobacco. The effect for the smoker is that the tobacco becomes milder, more smokeable and flavourful.

Filler Tobacco found in the middle of a cigar, the majority of the tobacco is classified as filler. This leaf is different from the Binder which surrounds it and the wrapper which wraps the outside of the cigar.

Foot The end of the cigar which is lit, opposite the end put in the mouth, is called the foot.

Habano A cigar made in Havana. This term has been extended to cigars made in Cuba in recent decades. The company responsible for marketing and distributing Cuban cigars globally is called HABANOS, which is derived from this term.

Head The end of a cigar placed in the mouth when smoking is called the head.

Humidor A box, jar or other container which is designed

to maintain a constant humidity, in this case for storing cigars.

Ligero A leaf grown near the top of the tobacco plant which becomes coarse, thick and extremely flavourful is called Ligero.

Long-filler A term for leaves placed in cigars which run from foot to head. These leaves are not cut short such as in *picadura* cigars.

Maduro Well-fermented tobacco leaves are called Maduro. There is some dispute about this word as it has taken on two definitions. One definition refers to heavily fermented leaf. The other definition refers to the dark colour that these leaves often assume.

Oscuro Dark, nearly black, coloured tobacco leaves, usually wrapper, are described as Oscuro.

Parejo The most common shape of cigar has straight, parallel sides and a rounded head. This is called Parejo, as compared with *figurado* cigars which have curved sides.

Priming When tobacco leaves are cut from the plant, they are grouped together by priming. Priming means cutting. But more specifically it refers to the group of leaves from one level of the plant which were cut and grouped together. These leaves are expected to have a similar taste due to their height on the plant.

Puro Meaning pure, Puro refers to a cigar whose tobacco was grown all in one place, usually referring to a country. A Cuban Puro is a cigar whose tobacco was all grown in Cuba.

Ring Gauge Refers to the width of the cigar, its diameter as expressed in 64ths of an inch. A cigar with a 46 ring gauge is 46/64 of an inch while a 64 ring gauge cigar is one inch across its diameter.

Shade Grown A term which refers to tobacco grown under a canopy of some kind. Usually this refers to wrapper leaf grown under muslin in order to give it an elastic quality free of blemishes.

Shoulder On a *parejo* cigar, the transition from the straight sides to the head is made by the cigar's shoulder. This refers to the rounded part of the cigar which forms this transition.

Sun-Grown Since all filler tobacco is grown in the sun, this term refers to wrapper leaf grown without a canopy.

Torcedor A cigar roller.

Index

143

144